# Praise for *The Fiefdom Syndrome*

"Turf wars and bureaucracy can undermine even the strongest corporate strategies. Drawing on lessons learned throughout his distinguished career, Bob describes innovative and practical ways to tackle this pervasive problem—and beat *The Fiefdom Syndrome*."

> **—Bill Gates,** chairman and chief software architect, Microsoft Corporation

"Bob Herbold's book identifies the causes, symptoms, and cures of one of the great diseases (scourges) that insidiously destroy large corporations in America (i.e., fiefdoms and bureaucracy)."

> **—Jamie Dimon,** chairman and CEO, Bank One Corporation

"I've seen Bob successfully tackle business challenges both at Procter & Gamble and at Microsoft. In *The Fiefdom Syndrome*, he identifies a critical business problem in the corporate world that very few have been able to solve—until now. This should be required reading across corporate America."

> **—James I. Cash Jr.,** James E. Robison Professor of Business Administration, Harvard University Graduate School of Business

"A vitally important business book. As Bob Herbold, longtime COO of Microsoft, makes clear, the battles over territory and turf stem from basic human behavior. Uncontrolled, they can be incredibly destructive, yet they are inherent in every organization. In *The Fiefdom Syndrome*, Herbold shows how fiefdoms can hamstring a company's operations, and how to break through them. I strongly urge people of all organizations, large and small, profit and non-profit, to read this book."

> **—John Chambers,** president and CEO, Cisco Systems

"Fiefdoms are the enemy of collaboration and external focus. They turn organizations inward and distract companies from customer needs and competitive realities. Bob Herbold gets to the heart of why fiefdoms exist and what leaders can do to overcome them. This is an important book for any leader who is responsible for sustained business growth."

> —**A. G. Lafley,** chairman, chief executive, and president, the Procter & Gamble Company

"The foundation of a successful organization is a team focused on common goals. With its thorough analysis and practical insights, this book will help you recognize, eliminate, and prevent the cancer of individual agendas."

> —**Michael Dell,** chairman, Dell Inc.

"*The Fiefdom Syndrome* is a must-read for any executive who faces the pervasive and crippling challenge of turf battles. All institutions need a clear, unified mission, and Bob Herbold's new book will help managers achieve it."

> —**Hank Paulson,** chairman & CEO, the Goldman Sachs Group, Inc.

"*The Fiefdom Syndrome* tackles a pervasive and seldom-discussed problem—namely, why organizations tend to become slow-footed, fragmented, and mediocre. Herbold provides valuable insights into cutting through the fiefdom syndrome, allowing you and your team to make the most of your talents, improve your organization, and avoid stalled careers."

> —**John Doerr,** partner, Kleiner Perkins Caufield & Byers

"Bob Herbold takes on the bureaucracy and turf battles that can undercut any company's agility—the kind of problems Sam Walton fought his whole life to overcome. I strongly recommend it."

—**Rob Walton,** chairman of the board, Walmart Stores, Inc.

"I have seen many organizations with strategy or profitability problems where the core issues blocking their progress are the types of fiefdom-like behaviors Bob describes. The reader will highly value the powerful, useful learnings in this book, told via great 'war stories' by a very experienced practitioner. I strongly recommend *The Fiefdom Syndrome.*"

—**Adrian Slywotzky,** author, *Value Migration, The Profit Zone,* and *The Art of Profitability*

"Fiefdoms, turf wars, and bureaucracy are often related to getting out of balance on centralization or decentralization. Bob Herbold provides valuable insights on how to achieve the proper balance and how to recognize and then avoid the pitfalls of decentralization that goes too far, i.e. fiefdoms."

—**Dick Kovacevich,** chairman and CEO, Wells Fargo & Company

"In this day and age, turf battles and bureaucracy are practically synonymous. As one who has seen these battles up close, both in public sector and private sector, I was intrigued by *The Fiefdom Syndrome.* Bob not only analyzes the causes; he offers compelling suggestions on how to overcome them. Whether you are in business, government, education, or the non-profits, I urge you to read this book, and more importantly take its advice and put it to good use."

—**Jack Kemp**

# Praise for *Seduced By Success*

"Seldom do you find a book with as many powerful, useful reminders that help you face up to reality and deal with problems. It becomes very clear why so many organizations fall behind and lose their way. I strongly urge you to read it."

> **—Grant L. Kelley,** principal & CEO, Colony Capital Asia

"This book rings painfully true. Bob Herbold demonstrates with clinical precision that a company's precipitate fall from grace can frequently be traced back to its time of greatest achievement. Before you get too depressed, however, take heart—he also gives you all the tools you need to avoid that ignominious fate. Anyone interested in sustained success should study it closely."

> **—Martin Sorrell,** chief executive officer, WPP Group PLC

"Bob Herbold gets to the heart of why successful organizations and individuals often go into a tailspin, and how this can be avoided. His thorough reviews of specific companies we all know make this a very useful book, and I highly recommend it."

> **—Indra K. Nooyi,** president & CEO, PepsiCo, Inc.

"*Seduced by Success* is a great book and should be compulsory reading for all managers. It's very instructive to read the detailed case studies showing how some successful companies lose their way, while others remain successful. Through these rich examples Bob Herbold shows how to sustain success."

> **—Koh Boon Hwee,** chairman, DBS Group Holdings/DBS Bank, Asia

# What's HOLDING You Back?

## TEN BOLD STEPS THAT DEFINE GUTSY LEADERS

Robert J. Herbold

**JB** JOSSEY-BASS
A Wiley Imprint
www.josseybass.com

Published by Jossey-Bass
A Wiley Imprint
989 Market Street, San Francisco, CA 94103-1741—www.josseybass.com

Readers should be aware that Internet Web sites offered as citations and/or sources for further information may have changed or disappeared between the time this was written and when it is read.

Limit of Liability/Disclaimer of Warranty: While the publisher and author have used their best efforts in preparing this book, they make no representations or warranties with respect to the accuracy or completeness of the contents of this book and specifically disclaim any implied warranties of merchantability or fitness for a particular purpose. No warranty may be created or extended by sales representatives or written sales materials. The advice and strategies contained herein may not be suitable for your situation. You should consult with a professional where appropriate. Neither the publisher nor author shall be liable for any loss of profit or any other commercial damages, including but not limited to special, incidental, consequential, or other damages.

Jossey-Bass books and products are available through most bookstores. To contact Jossey-Bass directly call our Customer Care Department within the U.S. at 800-956-7739, outside the U.S. at 317-572-3986, or fax 317-572-4002.

Jossey-Bass also publishes its books in a variety of electronic formats. Some content that appears in print may not be available in electronic books.

**Library of Congress Cataloging-in-Publication Data**
Herbold, Robert J.
  What's holding you back? : ten bold steps that define gutsy leaders / Robert J. Herbold.
    p. cm.
  Includes bibliographical references and index.
  ISBN 978-0-470-63901-6 (cloth); ISBN 978-0-470-93406-7 (ebk);
  ISBN 978-0-470-93407-4 (ebk); ISBN 978-0-470-93408-1 (ebk)
1. Decision making. 2. Leadership. I. Title.
  HD30.23.H48 2011
  658.4'092—dc22
                                                              2010043004
Printed in the United States of America
FIRST EDITION
HB Printing       10 9 8 7 6 5 4 3 2 1

*To Patricia*

# CONTENTS

# Introduction

E ffective leaders must be bold enough and brave enough to make tough choices. Sounds simple enough. Yet chances are that you have experienced a situation where, as a manager of a group (or department, division, or whole company), you know what you have to do, but you also know that these steps will be unpopular, or that the change is so significant or the idea so new and against the grain that many people will think you are doing the wrong thing. And, you reflect, you might be wrong—perhaps horrendously, embarrassingly so. People might lose their jobs. Your boss might not be happy. And so on.

A lot of managers face these tough issues and waffle, becoming paralyzed with indecision. They delay, analyze further, make massive compromises, ignore the whole thing, or employ any other tactic to avoid dealing with the tough situation. This lack of courage, this total inaction action, is what destroys companies.

Take, for instance, General Motors, which filed for bankruptcy on June 1, 2009. The world seemed shocked that a long-standing symbol of American commerce and manufacturing could fall so far, but the primary issues driving the company down were nothing new—in fact, they had been in place for more than twenty-five years. As far back as 1983, GM faced huge manufacturing inefficiencies when compared to the competition.[1] The Japanese had a cost advantage of approximately $1,500 to $2,000 over GM for a subcompact car.[2] In 2008, Toyota had a cost advantage over GM that was almost $1,400 per car.[3] In twenty-five years, nothing had really changed.

GM's problems over the twenty-five-year period were not just related to cost. Even in 1986, GM's shortcomings in manufacturing and design were widely known, and for the most part the company's cars were unexciting and very much alike.[4] This remained true for the next

1

two decades. In early 2009, just one out of forty-two cars in *Consumer Report*'s "Best in Class" new car ratings was a GM car.[5] In contrast, various Toyota models won eighteen of the forty-two ratings.[6] The era of GM's distinctive designs of the 1970s had long passed. GM's design issues had been obvious—and accepted—for years.

How was it that the talented managers of this global giant could stare at these problems for over a generation and do nothing about them? What was holding them back?

The company's core problem was lack of consistent, courageous leadership. When an organization faces a major challenge that threatens its competitiveness—and its very existence—the leaders must do something and do it fast to get them out of that mess, yet GM did nothing. Courage has been totally absent in the GM management ranks for decades.

███

The financial crisis of late 2008 and 2009 has put even more pressure on managers to face up to tough decisions and make them. As demand for products and services dropped on a global scale, those companies with courageous leadership, who kept their organizations lean, agile, and innovative, survived a whole lot better than those plagued by slow-moving, bureaucratic organizations.

Courageous management has real impact. Gutsy leaders are constantly making sure that their organization has a simple, understandable, clear game plan for the future. In addition, headcount is kept as low as possible, and processes are constantly simplified and standardized in order to minimize distractions.

Just as important, strong, courageous leaders create a culture that is curious, even paranoid about the future, to keep people always looking for new ways to help the company grow and improve. They make sure that decision making is crisp and accountability is clear. They constantly look for important new trends in consumer behavior and technology that they can use to their advantage. Once important change is planned, they reconfigure the organization to implement that change quickly and effectively.

Not only does this kind of results-oriented leadership keep the business fresh and alive, but when you face a crisis like the one the world saw in 2008 and 2009, the organization is far more agile and prepared to make the changes needed not only to survive but to win.

Tragically, during the financial crisis, we saw numerous companies in a variety of industries that struggled mightily while their competitors took bold, swift action to cope. For example, in the automobile business, Ford distinguished itself during this very tough period, as did Wells Fargo and J.P. Morgan Chase in the financial services sector. These three companies spotted the risks early and took very decisive actions. Those that suffered most just weren't used to constantly seeking out new plans to increase their effectiveness in changing environments. They typically left personnel in their current jobs way too long, which caused them to become stale and protective of current practices. They allowed excess headcount to exist. This consistently leads to organizational complexity, fragmented processes, and bloated costs.

Management that doesn't confront problems and make the necessary tough decisions to change typically ends up with a culture focused on pride in the past and the protection of old procedures. More often than not this leads to consensus decision making, in which no one thoroughly investigates an issue because he or she is not personally accountable for the results of the decision. Organizations with this kind of management usually get run over by new trends and new technology. They become insular and compartmentalized and incapable of initiating the kind of change required to meet major challenges, such as the financial crisis of 2008 and 2009.

The core issue we tackle in this book is the importance of hard-charging, gutsy leadership. It's tough to stay lean and agile as an organization. It's tough to constantly innovate and execute new, bright ideas that will increase the satisfaction and loyalty of your customers. But it can be done and you can do it. This book will show you how.

# 1

# The Big Issue

## Managers Lacking Courage to Make Tough Decisions

M any managers shy away from the tough decisions. Yet managers become leaders only when they lead, which means tackling the hard decisions head-on. In this chapter, we will explore the characteristics of tough decisions, the key reasons why many managers wimp out, and most important, the disastrous implications of such behavior. The rest of the book will provide you with ten useful principles you can use to avoid such problems.

To gain insight into just how important this topic is, let's take a look at a company that was brought close to the brink of bankruptcy because of weak leadership. Then, miraculously, a really strong, gutsy leader emerged, saved the franchise, and put it back into a leading position in its industry on a global scale.

## FIAT: A NEAR-DEATH EXPERIENCE

Founded in Turin, Italy, in 1899, Fiat emerged in the twentieth century as Italy's largest and most prestigious company. In the late 1980s and early 1990s, Fiat accounted for more than 50 percent market share in Italy's auto business. In fact, this company was so revered in Italy that whoever took on the role of the CEO was considered "a kind of mythical personage, somewhere between Pope and Prime Minister."[1]

Then, beginning in 1995, the Fiat Group experienced a rough financial patch that would last for ten years. In fact, some thought that Fiat was bound to "spiral into nothingness."[2] The company was suffering from excessive executive turnover, stifling bureaucracy, and unexciting cars. Why was this perennially successful company, which had been thriving for nearly a century, in such a state? Most analysts cited weak leadership throughout the company. Tough decisions were not being made, and as a result, a company that was once a national treasure was being run into the ground. In more detail, here are the key problems Fiat was facing due to poor leadership.

## Turnover and Confusion

Fiat has always been a family-run company, even though it is publicly traded. In 1999, one hundred years after Fiat was founded by Giovanni Agnelli, about a hundred descendents of the founder held 31 percent of the company.[3] The "family" took high interest in keeping control of Fiat, but it was a very messy task indeed. The grandson of the founder, also named Giovanni Agnelli but often called Gianni, was a long-standing chairman of the Fiat Group until 1996, when he became the honorary chairman until his death in January 2003.[4] Although board member Paolo Fresco served as chairman most of the time that Gianni was honorary chairman, Gianni was clearly the patriarch of the company and the family.

When Gianni died, his brother Umberto Agnelli became chairman, and Fresco retired. When Umberto suddenly died in 2004, there was somewhat of a family crisis. The family's only option was to make twenty-eight-year-old John Elkann, grandson of Gianni and Fiat board member since age twenty-two, the vice chairman to protect the family's interests, and to appoint close family friend, Luca Cordero di Montezelemolo, a thirty-plus-year employee and head of Fiat's Ferrari division, to be chairman.[5] It was clear to everyone that young Elkann was in charge, given the family's large shareholdings.

While this family version of musical chairs was going on, the business was suffering badly, and during the period from late 2001 to early 2004, the company had four different CEOs; most of them quickly becoming a casualty of the latest quarter's disastrous financial results. All four had been career Fiat employees for over twenty-five years. The fourth one left when Elkann was installed as vice chairman.

All of this handing off of the company among family members and career employees led Stephen Cheetham, an analyst at Stanford Bernstein Company, to remark that "Fiat isn't an automobile company; it's a national industrial conglomerate in crisis."[6] To illustrate the degree of confusion, in late 2002 Paolo Fresco, chairman of Fiat's board of directors, who at age sixty-nine had been looking forward to retirement, found himself immersed in board chaos. Owning 31 percent of Fiat, the Agnelli family had tried to oust Fresco as chairman, a post he had assumed in 1998. Gabriele Galateri, who had been Fiat Group CEO for only five months, had just quit. In December 2002, after a raucous board meeting, Fresco wound up as both chairman and CEO, instead of sailing off into retirement sunset, because that arrangement resolved a family and board power struggle.[7]

During this period, rather than looking both inside and outside Fiat, and thoughtfully and carefully selecting highly experienced and successful executives for key positions such as chairman and CEO, Fiat seemed to be appointing the most convenient alternative, reflecting family wishes and only looking inside.

### Excessive Layers of Management

By 2002, Fiat had become an excessively large and bloated company with almost one hundred thousand workers.[8] This was due to overstaffing and organizational fragmentation, which led to a thick hierarchical management culture, filled with midlevel managers and bureaucracy. The CEO of the company hired Jack Welch to help Fiat figure out how to speed things up. Welch's assessment: "Fiat suffers from too many layers of management and a consensus culture that protects under-performers."[9] Fiat was burdened with "a very hierarchal, status-driven, relationship-driven organization," wrote Stefan Faris in *Fortune*.[10]

### Ugly Cars and Plummeting Market Shares

Fiat's share of the Italian car market dropped from 52 percent at the start of the 1990s to below 28 percent in 2003.[11] Fiat was making cars the public didn't much like and that were too expensive for their class. For example, Fiat introduced a compact car called Stilo that did poorly in the marketplace because consumers thought it was ugly and believed it cost too much; because of this, the Stilo was a disappointment, selling less than 50 percent of what Fiat expected.[12] Courageous leaders drive hard to provide their customers with great value—exciting products at attractive prices. Such courage was lacking at Fiat.

## Bad Branding and Poor Quality

No one seemed responsible for brand image at Fiat, leading to "boxy and uninspired" models.[13] Unfortunately, when you're trying to sell boring products, about the only marketing tool left for generating sales is to reduce prices. Weak product followed by price cuts causes your brand reputation to atrophy further, setting off a vicious cycle. This is what happened to Fiat.

In the rush to get products to market, Fiat didn't test its products for consumer appeal—a crucial step, and one that takes place preferably before the product is in the marketplace. Such testing enables leaders to act immediately when defects and weaknesses are detected. At Fiat, there was no leader demanding the necessary rigor in the product development process.

During this period, another product issue with which Fiat was struggling was quality. The small-engine Fiats of the 1980s had poor reliability.[14] The negative word of mouth caused Fiat to take another hit; Fiat's reputation for poor-quality cars led to the joke suggesting that the name Fiat stood for *F*ix *I*t *A*gain, *T*ony.[15]

## Duplication

Massive complexity and duplication throughout the company also meant that Fiat's costs were high. Each of Fiat's auto brands, Fiat, Alpha Romeo, and Lancia, worked separately on its own brand development, engineering, component design, and market analysis. The Fiat Stilo and the Alpha Romeo Model 149 were very similar cars with similar performance, yet they shared no components. Neither capitalized on information the other turned up. So Fiat wound up with nineteen completely different platforms on which it built different models and brands.[16] For example, the product development groups were so independent that only two of the nineteen used the same heating, ventilating, and air-conditioning system. Weak leaders had let the different organizations go about their business and do whatever they wanted. They were not taking advantage of economies of scale and information sharing.

**Lack of Focus**

Although Fiat's core business was automobiles, over the years it diluted its focus by getting into a mind-numbingly diverse set of businesses: insurance, banking, farm and construction equipment, publishing, energy, trucks, aircraft engines, and Formula One automobile racing with Ferrari.[17] It was as if Fiat had become a holding company for ventures that caught the Agnelli family's fancy. Strong leaders get into only those businesses in which they are intent on becoming a major player. In general, there is no way that a diverse set of interests can lead to the kind of focus required for a company to be successful. Fiat violated that concept.

## THE RESULTING FINANCIAL CATASTROPHE

By 2004, the Fiat Group was close to bankruptcy, with a negative cash flow of over $1 billion.[18] It had recorded record losses of $1.5 billion and needed to raise over $1 billion in twelve months to pay off maturing bonds. The financial community was very concerned with Fiat's ability to take on even more debt.[19] It was borrowing heavily against its receivables, pushing its total obligations to almost $13 billion.[20] By mid-2004, "the ailing automaker had racked up more than $12 billion in losses over five years and was headed for insolvency," according to *Business Week*.[21]

Back in 2000, when Fiat's liquidity crisis was beginning to emerge, Fiat's chairman, Paolo Fresco, signed a controversial contract with

GM.[22] GM agreed to take a 20 percent position in the Fiat Group. GM seemed to have thought this long-standing European company had a strong future and would quickly pull itself out of any financial problems. The deal essentially gave Fiat the right to "put" the whole company to GM in the future at a fair market price at the time of the put.[23] For Fiat's leaders to sign any such agreement meant that their confidence in the company's future was weak, because they were basically creating a way out. The intent on GM's part was not very clear. It may have had interest in Fiat's small car business in Europe as a means of increasing market share and production capacity in that segment and area.

## THE OVERALL ASSESSMENT

In 2004, the prevailing wisdom in the auto industry was that Fiat had "the talent, knowledge, and skills, but it lacked leadership."[24] As responsibility fell from family member to family member, none individually had the guts or experience to step up to provide the courageous leadership required to run a large corporation like Fiat. This lack of committed, courageous leadership left Fiat floundering.

## FIAT: AT LAST ... A GUTSY LEADER

Although the Fiat Group had multiple problems as a company, none of its individual problems were that complex. By far, Fiat's largest, most complex problem was the lack of strong leadership. Fortunately, the company's board of directors finally realized this. In June 2004, they hired a courageous leader, Sergio Marchionne, as CEO. Born in Italy but raised in Toronto, Marchionne had a strong track record as a turnaround specialist. He was also an outsider to the auto industry, which many regarded as a major plus.

## Putting Top Talent in Key Jobs

After a couple of months of getting oriented to the company, Marchionne moved into action. He began by firing numerous Fiat managers he thought were obstructing change and brought in new talent with automotive industry experience.[25] For example, he convinced Stefan Ketter, the former head of quality at VW's U.S. subsidiary, to join his team. He also recruited Karl-Heinz Kaldfell, a former BMW veteran and CEO of Rolls-Royce Motor Cars Ltd., to run Alpha Romeo. Herbert Demel, a former Audi executive, was hired to overhaul Fiat's industrial operations and try to lower its cost base.

Marchionne also found high-quality emerging talent within Fiat and quickly put those individuals in key jobs. For example, soon after arriving at Fiat, he spotted Antonio Baravalle, then marketing manager at Alpha Romeo. Baravalle recalls being asked by Marchionne, "Tell me what was wrong with what you did in the past."[26] Baravalle explained that he hadn't thought big enough; he had set his market share targets too low behind Alpha Romeo's push into Britain, causing the organization to field only a modest marketing effort. Marchionne was looking for objectivity and a high energy level. He liked what he saw in Baravalle and put him in charge of Lancia.

It takes courage to move into a new organization and, after quickly assessing what needs to be done, grab the people you think can do it, and put them into the key jobs. No doubt some people get bruised in the process, but as long as the leader's objectives are clear to the troops, they usually end up applauding the fact that the organization has a plan and is tackling it with gusto.

## Tackling Excess Layers and Personnel

As Marchionne saw it, "This was a very hierarchical, status-driven, relationship-driven organization. All that got blown up in July 2004."[27] Within months of arrival, he began chopping out layers. A 10 percent reduction among the twenty thousand white-collar workers in

Fiat headquarters was announced. This was a big shock to a workforce which assumed that a job at Fiat was for life, and was unaccustomed to outsiders taking key positions or emerging leaders being promoted quickly.[28]

Marchionne set about to simplify the complexity generated by the company's nineteen platforms independently developed across Fiat's many brands. Hard-charging Harald Wester was hired in 2004 as head of engineering. He was from Magna Steyr, an Austrian automobile manufacturer, and he quickly announced that 85 percent of Fiat's models would be produced on just four platforms by 2010.[29] He also announced that models of the same size would share two-thirds of their components, most of which are not visible to the customer. His view was that "you cannot survive with small steps, you need to leapfrog to put yourself in a state-of-the-art position as soon as possible."[30] Nothing was going to hold Wester back.

### Innovating While Killing What Doesn't Work

Although not a "car guy," Marchionne aggressively innovated new models for Fiat, such as the Fiat Grand Punto. Also, under his leadership the Fiat Panda achieved four years of increasing sales. This was due to a strong product development effort, leading to a sequence of new features and upgrades and resulting in such cars as the Panda Cross, a 4-by-4 version of the Panda that also had SUV features and was the most popular of the Panda series.[31]

He also oversaw the contemporary remake of the Fiat 500, a model from the 1960s. Launched in September 2006, it went head-to-head with BMW's Mini. The car was a huge hit in Europe, with sales of nearly a quarter million between July 2007 and June 2008.[32] The new Fiat 500 reminded the Italians of a simpler era, just as BMW's Mini did for the BMW franchise. Its distinctive styling was in contrast to some of the "ordinary" Fiat models of the recent past.

While supporting innovation, Marchionne also quickly killed off projects that he viewed as lacking big impact, even in late stages of product development. For example, he stopped production of the Bravo because he wanted a better-looking, more exciting car.[33]

He then demanded that the redesigned Bravo be developed in half the usual time.

## Getting out of the GM Deal

In early 2005, with just eight months under his belt as CEO of Fiat, Marchionne was able to negotiate a $2 billion payment from General Motors to cancel the "put" Fiat had bargained for in 2000, which would have required GM, at Fiat's discretion, to buy Fiat at the current market price. The automotive industry experts were frankly amazed that "against all expectations, Mr. Marchionne managed to wring $2 billion from GM in return for ending the partnership."[34] I suspect that GM at that point didn't think Marchionne could pull Fiat out of its disastrous tailspin, and didn't want to be forced to add Fiat to its long list of horrendous problems.

Taking those funds, Marchionne continued to restructure Fiat, cutting staff and management layers, reengineering how work was done at the company, and launching a series of what eventually proved to be very successful models. Whereas previous leaders of Fiat had used the GM deal as the ultimate crutch to fall back on, Marchionne's attitude was exactly the opposite. He was anxious to get rid of the deal as soon as possible and restore Fiat to its previous glory.

## Setting Big Goals

At the November 2006 Fiat financial analyst meeting, Marchionne described an aggressive plan to boost Fiat into becoming one of the world's top-performing mass market automakers by 2010, consisting of a series of product moves projected to increase sales volume by eight hundred thousand vehicles and move Fiat's European market share from 8 percent in late 2006 to 11 percent. Given these plans and his performance leading Fiat during his two years as CEO, the financial analysts were impressed. Marchionne had already managed to save Fiat from very nearly becoming bankrupt. If he could truly bring his new plans for 2010 to fruition, "his overhaul of Fiat would rank as the most impressive turnaround in the history of the auto industry," according to *Business Week*.[35]

To preserve capital, Marchionne aggressively pushed for partnerships abroad in China, India, Russia, and Turkey, manufacturing Fiat-branded cars and selling them through local dealers.[36] By mid-2008, Marchionne was investigating plans for reintroducing Fiat in the U.S. market, which it had left in 1983.[37]

## THE IMPACT

Marchionne's strong leadership at Fiat generated quick results.[38] In 2006, Fiat returned to profitability for the first time since 2000. Revenues reached $31.1 billion, up 35 percent from 2005. Trading profits moved from a loss of $332 million in 2005 to a profit of $384 million in 2006. The Fiat Group announced that in 2007 it would pay its first dividend in five years.

Things continued to improve for Fiat after that incredibly successful year of 2006. In fact, the stock price moved from a low point of $7 per share when Marchionne joined the company to over $30 a share in the last six months of 2007. In the third quarter of 2008, the global financial crisis began to take its toll on Fiat, as it did on all auto companies. Business slowed, and Fiat's stock price was pummeled, down 60 percent from April to December 2008. But compared to both Chrysler and GM, who were driven into bankruptcy, and to Ford, which was down 75 percent, Fiat survived fairly well.

Being one of the few relatively healthy auto companies in spring 2009, Fiat offered to acquire a 35 percent stake in Chrysler as it emerged from bankruptcy, in exchange for Fiat technology only, no cash.[39] The deal was completed within a few months, enabling Chrysler's continued existence. Most industry experts speculate that Marchionne may eventually use the Chrysler deal as Fiat's entrée into the U.S. market via the Chrysler dealerships and service operations in the United States.

Fiat exemplified weak leadership in the late 1990s to mid-2004. But when Sergio Marchionne came on board, we saw the reverse. His courageous leadership turned the company around, simply by quickly grasping the situation and making the tough decisions needed to fix the problems.

# WHY MANAGERS DON'T MAKE TOUGH DECISIONS

Fiat got into its problems because of behavior I see over and over in managers at all levels: namely, shying away from the tough decisions that can make the difference between mediocrity and success. Failure to make such decisions occurs all the time, at all levels in organizations. But it is especially damaging during difficult financial times. Let's review what tough decisions are, why people often shy away from them, and what happens when they do.

## The Nature of Tough Decisions

The more responsibility a manager assumes, the greater the likelihood that he or she will face tough decisions characterized by one or more of the following traits:

- *No ideal option.* For many tough problems, there is no perfect path to improvement, solution, or innovation. This means that the decision maker must make trade-offs and choices. The worst option is to do nothing: you pass up the chance of improving things, and doing nothing leads to poor morale and a culture with no sense of urgency.
- *Lack of data.* For some decisions, there are issues for which no valid data exist or can be generated to significantly reduce risk. For example, this is often the case in setting staffing levels, deciding how to organize your group, or selecting a strategy from a set of conceptually different options, because there is no one "correct" answer. You are going to have to use some judgment based on experience, input from others, and your intuition.
- *Guaranteed disappointment.* There is almost never one solution that will please everyone. The big trap here is to endlessly seek compromises as a way of gaining the support of those affected. This just eats up time and weakens the impact of any eventual decision.

- *Long-term perspective needed.* Although a short-term, temporary solution may exist, the courageous leader demands that a longer-term perspective be taken. Many managers give in to an expeditious short-term fix instead of embracing the pain and hard work demanded by the correct long-term decision.

Unfortunately, when faced with the kind of tough decisions outlined here, many managers immediately start contemplating the downsides of confronting the problem. Let's take a look at why this kind of hesitation and fear occurs.

## Why Do Managers Wimp Out?

When managers fail to provide courageous leadership on tough issues, it is usually for one or more of the following reasons. These managers are

- *Avoiding conflict.* Knowing that not everyone will agree, some managers would rather compromise or do nothing than clearly state, after adequate study, where they come out on an issue and why, and then exercise their authority and make a decision.
- *Striving for certainty.* Many managers don't want to risk being wrong, so instead of taking action in a timely fashion, they continue searching for new data or theories that will unequivocally support their decision.
- *Avoiding a career risk.* Some people fear that if they take action and things go badly, their careers will be jeopardized or they will offend colleagues who will hold some sway over their careers in the future.
- *Lacking self-confidence.* Unfortunately some managers are simply too timid to take the lead and make tough decisions because they are uncomfortable trusting their own views. They often prefer not to make a decision at all when there isn't universal agreement.
- *Lacking a sense of urgency.* When things are going well, many managers can become complacent and are often reluctant to shake things up by taking risks. Their attitude is, what's the hurry? Things are

going along just fine. We have our challenges, but let's not rush into things.

- *Protecting their turf.* Some individuals become too comfortable in their jobs and fear that any change may render them vulnerable. They could lose status or be put out of a job; their lack of varied experiences would be revealed, or it could become clear just how out-of-date they are regarding technology.

## The Implications

There are huge implications when managers lack the courage to make the tough decisions. The problems to which this sort of behavior can lead usually fall into one of the following two categories:

1. *Operational complexity.* Weak leaders often lack the courage to turn down the never-ending requests for more manpower; their failure to do so results in excess personnel. Organizational fragmentation (various groups going off in separate directions) and nonstandardized processes emerge as the manager fears confronting and denying the endless requests of groups wanting to do their own thing. Ever-increasing bureaucracy and complexity are the results.
2. *Lack of innovation.* In dealing with new ideas and change, insecure or inexperienced managers often seek the safety of consensus-oriented decision making, thus suffocating innovation. Often there are no clear goals regarding innovation, and the qualification process for new ideas is random. Weak leadership also often causes a lack of clarity regarding who is responsible for spotting key trends and innovating accordingly.

## What to Do About It

The key question is, How can managers avoid such problems and significantly improve their ability to be courageous, gutsy leaders? The truth is, you are probably never going to turn the inherently timid person into a naturally charismatic, hard-charging leader. But all managers can learn ten fundamental principles that will enable them to spot what needs to be done, and to provide the leadership to make it happen. I based these ten principles on my forty years of business experience, and the remainder of this book focuses on describing them in detail and providing rich, specific examples from the marketplace that make the principles come alive.

# 2

## PRINCIPLE I

# Devise a Demanding Game Plan to Confront Reality

It's exciting to be the leader of an organization. It gives you the chance to have some real impact on the efficiency and effectiveness of what the group is doing. The exhilarating part of being a leader is diving in and figuring out exactly what is going well and what isn't, and how you can put together a demanding game plan that will improve the group's overall contribution to the organization. By a demanding game plan, I am referring to an aggressive and clear vision, the selection of the right strategies to fulfill the vision, and proper, well-defined measures of success.

The tough part about implementing change is that most people within any organization fear it. They are not sure how large-scale change will affect their jobs. They may perceive it as an indication that the work they're currently doing isn't good enough, and become defensive. A real change agent is typically going to run into some resistance within the organization. However, a strong leader doesn't let this stand in his way. Instead he tries to alleviate those fears by making it clear that there is big opportunity to improve the way the group works and how it contributes to the organization. He is transparent about the motives for the change and the expected gains, as well as about how it will affect those within the group. All this requires a fair amount of nerve on the part of the leader. He needs to confront his own fear of the internal resistance. And he needs to work to engage the troops so that they will share the excitement in improving the organization.

It's often said that it's easier to manage smaller companies than larger ones. One of the reasons for this is that with a smaller company, a game plan will usually present itself more obviously, and if it's not implemented properly and with a sense of urgency, it is more likely that the company's survival will be at risk. The clarity of what needs to be done, and done quickly, can be a huge advantage.

With larger companies, particularly successful ones, managers will often just accept that some of the divisions will be up and some will be down. And if one is down, it may cause worry, but the urgency generally won't be as great as if that division were a small company in and of itself and its very existence were being threatened. Good leaders, regardless of whether they are in a small or large organization, create a sense of urgency. When things aren't going well, they will implement a focused and demanding game plan to achieve significant improvement.

So how can you achieve the kind of crystal-clear direction necessary to create and implement a game plan that will ultimately lead to exciting innovation and operational excellence? As noted earlier, three things must be in place: (1) a clear vision with impact, (2) aggressive strategies to achieve that vision, and (3) a defined way of measuring success. The remainder of this chapter focuses on these three things, giving examples of companies that have successfully implemented a game plan and of some that have failed, but most important, it will detail how you can successfully establish these three things in your own organization.

## A CLEAR VISION WITH IMPACT

While working at Microsoft as the chief operating officer, I saw an excellent example of a leader putting together a demanding game plan. In 1995, the Internet was emerging as an incredibly powerful new tool, changing the way people were doing business and living their lives. For a period of about three months, Bill Gates orchestrated a lively dialogue with the key technical people at the company regarding what Microsoft should be doing to take full advantage of the Internet.

This active dialogue culminated in Gates's announcement of a demanding game plan for Microsoft and the Internet. He laid out the architecture of what eventually became Microsoft's Internet Explorer browser. He also announced the formation of a new organization headed up by Brad Silverberg to build and launch the browser. Key personnel were handpicked by Silverberg and Gates for the leadership positions in this new organization. After discussions with Silverberg and the new team, Gates selected the target date for the browser to be launched and a date for achieving a 10 percent market share among browsers. In addition, Gates set a specific goal of winning, within twelve months of introduction, 90 percent of the product reviews in the technical press regarding the performance of Internet Explorer versus other browsers. Equally impressive was the fact that all those goals were achieved. The thing that amazed me at the time was just how clear and specific Gates made the desired outcomes. He created a masterful, clear, and demanding game plan.

Another business leader who benefited from the clarity of his vision was Jack Welch, the chairman and CEO of General Electric from 1981 to 2001. He was famous for asking the heads of the key product divisions at GE to achieve either the number one or number two market share position in their particular industry. This clear, concise vision made it very obvious what these individuals needed to do. It caused the GE division heads to work aggressively to find out what it was that was holding them back if they weren't in that number one or number two spot. People also knew there would be consequences for failure. Welch made it clear that he had no qualms about replacing division heads if the vision was not attained in a reasonable amount of time. With that kind of crisp direction and sense of urgency, people tend to get to work very quickly on developing a demanding game plan for fixing problems and getting things growing.[1]

Whereas it's exciting to be part of an organization that has a clear vision and is progressing forward, it's exasperating to be in an organization where the boss is clearly floundering and nothing exciting is going on to improve the organization. Surprisingly, this happens all the time. Just think about General Motors over the last twenty-five years. Its cars lacked pizzazz, as evidenced by the demise of Oldsmobile and Pontiac. Its quality was not up to the competition, as measured annually by such firms as J.D. Power.[2] In the United States, GM needed to move to a nonunion labor arrangement like that of the U.S. manufacturing facilities of its key competitor, Toyota. For twenty-five years it seemed to stagger along, proud as ever, while its market share shrunk nearly every year—from 50 percent in the late 1970s to 20 percent when it went bankrupt in 2009.

Another company that had big problems launching a vision for the future was Vodafone, the mobile phone giant. Vodafone's problems were at the highest levels of the company, but the lessons are just as applicable to first-level managers in an organization. In February 2006, Vodafone Group announced that it wouldn't meet its quarterly profit targets, and that instead of quarterly revenue growth in the 6 to 9 percent range, it expected the range to be 5 to 6.5 percent. But the big shock came when Vodafone revealed that its assets were overvalued by an estimated $49 billion, the primary reason being that it never achieved the anticipated impact of its acquisition of Germany's Mannesmann in 2000. On the day of the announcement, Vodafone's stock dropped by 3 percent. The most unnerving thing for investors was that Vodafone had no clear vision of how it intended to get out of its mess. And so, according to the British financial group Standard Life Investments, the market "lost confidence in the company's global strategy."[3]

The core job of a leader in any organization is to quickly and accurately assess the current situation and any vulnerabilities and opportunities the organization may have. The leader must then lay out a demanding game plan—an exciting vision of positive, significant impact—and share that vision with all employees and stakeholders. Also, it should be clear that the leader stands ready to modify that plan at any moment, given new learning. The absence of such a vision on the part of Vodafone's leadership was clearly the most unsettling factor in this early 2006 profit warning.

Seven years earlier in 1999, Vodafone had embarked on a local and regional phone company acquisition spree, totaling $300 billion in expenditures. The sum total of all its effort was 179 million customers in twenty-seven countries, but Vodafone had difficulty incorporating all of these new acquisitions into the business because it had no clear game plan.[4]

If you don't have a game plan, critics will emerge from the sidelines to give you advice. Vodafone shareholders, such as Standard Life, suggested that it sell off its underperforming Japanese business as well as its 45 percent stake in Verizon Wireless in the United States and give the proceeds to the shareholders.[5] Dean Bubley, founder of Disruptive Analysis, a London consulting firm, thought the problem was technology, and that Vodafone should partner with or acquire a fixed-line operator.[6] Thomas Husson, mobile analyst at Jupiter Research, suggested it should "keep generating new revenue streams to compensate for the decline in voice revenues" and set up customer care centers in its existing shops to better promote its services and show how to use its products.[7] John Strand, CEO of Strand Consult, a wireless consulting company in Copenhagen, thought Vodafone should focus on cutting costs.[8] The suggestions went on and on, but at bottom, Vodafone was at fault for not having an aggressive, clear, and motivating vision for the future. Quick action should have been in the works immediately after the February 2006 profit warning, but not much changed.

At the end of 2006, Vodafone took a few significant steps, but still hadn't laid out a clear vision. Because the company had always struggled in Japan, it sold its 97 percent share in Vodafone Japan to Softbank, a Japanese technology company, in a move generally regarded as positive.[9] And although during 2007 the stock moved from the high $20s to the mid-$30s, this gain was short lived, and by mid-2008, it was down to the mid-$20s, a far cry from the high $50s of the late 1990s. CEO Arun Sarin stepped down in June 2008.

Vodafone illustrates how with tenure comes complacency and defensiveness. When leaders are in place for a long time, or when a company is well established, they can find it difficult to perceive floundering or lack of vision. As a leader, you need to recognize that you may be subject to these effects; to combat them, adopt the following practices:

- *Objectively analyze and face reality.* Be probing. At all times, question and analyze your situation to identify issues and opportunities. This is true if you are a CEO managing a whole corporation or just a new leader of a small group. You must constantly work to understand your customers (be they inside or outside your company), how they see you, and how you can improve. It can be quite challenging to be objective and face the reality of your organization's situation, but without an honest assessment, you can't develop an appropriate game plan.

- *Draft an exciting vision.* The key question of any analysis is, What change do we want to see happen? The answer will be your vision. With Internet Explorer, Bill Gates wanted to launch it by a certain date to have a 10 percent market share a specific number of months thereafter.

- *Get feedback.* Once the vision and rationale are drafted, get it in the hands of those it will affect, seek feedback, and listen carefully. We're not talking about getting 100 percent agreement. That would be a huge mistake. We're talking about getting input and objectively analyzing that input. Some of the feedback will be superficial, and some people will oppose your ideas just because they fear change. You need to be objective enough and forceful enough to reject such input and explain why you're doing so, but open minded enough to recognize good feedback and incorporate it. The goal in this step is to fine-tune the vision and gain valuable input and perspective that will improve it.

- *Take action.* Announce your new vision. Explain why you are choosing that direction, what will be different, and what you think the impact will be. You need to motivate people and create excitement.

Not everyone will agree, especially if the new vision means job changes or eliminations. Change is always threatening. If dissenters persist after you explain the what and why, you'll need to deal with them. Either they join up and pitch in to the best of their ability, or you must work with them to find something else for them to do inside or outside the company.

- *Be continuously critical.* As you implement your vision, you need to keep the same process of analysis going to critique it. What's working and not working as you move forward? Continue to get feedback throughout implementation, change what needs to be changed, and start over again if necessary. Constant ongoing improvement will make all the difference in the effort's eventual success.
- *Repeat the process.* Once the vision is implemented, guess what? You get to start the whole process all over again, seeking out the next far-reaching goal for your group.

This sequence of analyze, draft, critique, act, critique again, and start over is basically the continuous improvement model of Japanese Total Quality and the foundation of Six Sigma. The problem is that most leaders over time become sloppy and complacent, and lose their zest for change-oriented continuous improvement. Their attitude evolves to one of "My organization is running pretty well. What's all the fuss about?"

There is nothing worse than a leadership vacuum. It invites chaos and speculation that distract and unnerve employees. At all times, leaders need to have a vision they make public while remaining willing to listen to new input and modify that vision.

## AGGRESSIVE STRATEGIES TO ACHIEVE YOUR VISION

Once you have the vision nailed down, the next step is figuring out how to achieve it. You must not only create strategies but also deal with employees who may get worried about what those strategies mean in relation to their current jobs. It's not unusual to find more effort going into turning up roadblocks of all sorts than into implementing the vision. But with the right focus and determination, it can be done.

Let's take a look at two companies where the leaders had clear visions and set up very specific strategies to achieve them.

Hyundai is an organization that has made huge progress in the automobile business since the late 1990s. Hyundai's is a surprising and positive story about the impact a leader can have when his or her goals are clear and the organization is successfully reconfigured to achieve them.

In the late 1990s, Hyundai was the twelfth-largest global manufacturer of automobiles, just starting to make its move to sell cars in the United States. In those early days in the United States, the company had huge problems with quality. The culture of Hyundai during the 1980s and 1990s was basically to sell as many cars as possible. All other aspects of the business, such as quality and styling, were at best a second priority. This mentality really hurt the company when it came to the U.S. market.

Hyundai Motor Company was established in 1967 by Chung Ju-Yung. Chung Ju-Yung's son, Chung Mong-Koo, worked at a variety of positions within the auto company, patiently waiting for his turn to run it. In 1999, leadership of the auto company was finally put in the hands of Chung Mong-Koo by his father, who was chairman of the group.

Chung Mong-Koo knew there were serious quality problems, because there had always been lots of customer complaints. It was his vision for Hyundai to become one of the top five selling automobile companies in the world. Objectively analyzing its issues led Chung to rally Hyundai around a huge push for product quality and reliability. These were, Chung correctly believed, the secret to achieving major growth. He began to organize the company around the new strategy. The first step Chung took was to replace the top executives, who had finance backgrounds, with engineers. Chung then set the company's sights on beating Toyota in J.D. Power's quality rankings.[10] Chung also knew the importance of quantifying progress toward greater quality and reliability.

Next, Chung hired several engineers to work closely with J.D. Power in order to fully understand Hyundai's quality problems and how the company compared to the world's best automobile companies. He made sure that his group of engineers spent time in America studying road conditions and driving habits, so as to understand firsthand the challenges consumers faced, as well as how to compete in America with the very best and most successful automobile manufacturers.[11]

Chung established a high-profile quality department within Hyundai, staffed with strong performers, and had this group report directly to him. This sent a strong message to the troops regarding just how serious the company was in driving up quality. He set up mechanisms so that employees could get their ideas to management's attention and have them acted on quickly. At the Hyundai factory near Seoul, in the initial stages of the drive to improve the company, workers came up with more than twenty-five thousand ideas, of which about 30 percent were adopted.[12]

Throughout this major effort, the yardstick was the J.D. Power survey, a fact made quite public throughout the company. Also, consumer complaints were carefully tracked and given significant publicity within the company in order to create awareness of the importance of customer satisfaction. Chung initiated a weekly quality meeting where a group of about fifty key engineers and high-level personnel, designers, suppliers, and manufacturing managers spent three hours reviewing the facts and figures on the quality of the cars coming off the line. They also spent time examining specific models for problems.

To emphasize the importance of getting things perfect, Chung didn't hesitate to delay the development and rollout of new models if there were quality issues. During the launch of the Sonata, drive-test engineers uncovered a rattle coming from the Sonata front doors and spent two months trying to figure out where it was coming from and how to stop it. Eventually, the plastic strip at the bottom of the door was replaced by a polymer compound strip that ended the rattle. As noted by Dawn Hyung Jo, manager of the Asian quality control department, if the same problem had occurred five years earlier, "we'd probably leave it."[13] Chung made sure that his vision of leading in quality and reliability was clear and widely understood in the company. He also made clear that this was the path to becoming one of the largest auto producers in the world. Employees all knew that their performance in these areas was being tracked. This caused the value system of Hyundai to shift.

Hyundai put special attention on consumer feedback. Early in the launch of the Hyundai Santa Fe, owners complained of wind noise. Engineers quickly determined that the shape of the side-view mirrors and the cross bar on the vehicle's luggage rack were causing the problem. These and any other issues consumers raised about the Santa Fe were quickly addressed and fixed. The vehicle's J.D. Power quality score went from 149 problems per hundred vehicles in its initial study in 2003 to just 93 in 2004. Another measure watched closely at Hyundai was repurchase rates. By 2004, the company had improved that statistic significantly; specifically, four out of every five Hyundai cars were traded in for another Hyundai. As a further demonstration of its commitment to quality, Hyundai began offering an unheard of 10-year, 100,000-mile warranty on its automobiles.[14]

All this focus on quality and reliability led to extraordinary improvements. In 2004, Hyundai achieved a virtual tie with quality leaders Toyota and Honda in the J.D. Power annual study of initial vehicle quality.[15] *Consumer Reports* reported in its April 2004 issue that the Hyundai Sonata was the most reliable car on the road, with just two problems per hundred vehicles. That is, objectively, astounding quality.

Because its leadership set a specific vision and created aggressive strategies to achieve that vision, Hyundai went from twelfth-largest car manufacturer in the late 1990s to sixth largest in 2006, and doubled the U.S. business from 2002 to 2007. In television advertising, the company now compares its cars to top-of-the-line luxury cars, such as BMW.[16] Clearly, Hyundai is a terrific example of the power of a clear vision and strategies.

Let's review another useful example. In early 2001, Gillette was a company in serious trouble, having missed its earnings promise to Wall Street for an astounding fourteen consecutive quarters. Sales and earnings hadn't grown for five years. Whereas the company had been one of the premier performers in the consumer products industry in the early to mid-1990s, now "two-thirds of Gillette's products were losing share"; clearly the management had let the company drift aimlessly.[17] In the prior three years, Gillette's stock had dropped 30 percent. In 1999, halfway through its painful decline, the company replaced the CEO, Alfred Zeien, with Mike Hawley, a thirty-five-plus-year Gillette employee. It didn't work. During Hawley's first eighteen months as CEO, sales and market shares continued to soften, and earnings did not recover. It was time for yet another new leader; board member and investor Warren Buffett was signaling his strong desire for an outsider.[18]

In February 2001, the Gillette board of directors finally made a bold move and hired Jim Kilts, an experienced turnaround artist, to fix the problem. Kilts excelled at quickly developing clear, concise visions and strategies that, if mastered, would lead to business success, and he had done it over and over at places like Kraft and Nabisco. As Warren Buffett commented, "If you listen to Jim analyze a business situation, you get absolutely no baloney."[19]

During the six weeks prior to stepping into his new job as Gillette CEO, Kilts launched a massive effort to study Gillette, reviewing the financials in depth, including industry reviews. He traveled extensively with sales personnel, worked with manufacturing personnel, and dove into Gillette's advertising and consumer comments.

Following this thorough analysis, Kilts quickly came forward with a document he titled "Escaping the Circle of Doom."[20] The essence of his analysis was that Gillette had been consistently unrealistic about what it was going to achieve, leading to such disappointments as missing quarterly profit estimates fourteen straight times. The memo was incredibly frank, and he shared it with the company broadly. Employees were shocked, but Kilts was simply facing the reality of the situation and telling employees that they must face reality also.

After giving his crash course on what Gillette had been up to and receiving feedback from employees, he went to work on putting Gillette's revenue, profits, and market shares back on a healthy growth track in all divisions. At the start of each quarter, division heads were required to review their progress, strategic goals, and measures of progress, and to explain it all to Kilts. Each week they were required to submit a brief memo outlining their progress. At the end of the quarter, Kilts would give them each a grade between 0 and 100 on the results during that quarter. The individual's pay, any possible promotions, and continuing employment were based on that grade. Kilts made it very clear that anything consistently below 80 was unacceptable.[21]

Kilts used industry benchmarks in developing individual strategies with his managers. Staff departments (for example, finance and HR) had to meet or beat the industry average on various benchmarks, such as budgets as a percentage of revenue. For operating divisions, goals with regard to product innovation, cost, revenue, percentage of sales in new items, and profit were agreed on with the top management. These were the kinds of things Kilts evaluated at the end of each quarter.

The turnaround Gillette made by the end of 2002 was frankly remarkable. The company's free cash flow had increased by 60 percent from early 2001, and a debt of $1.8 billion had been paid off. The stock price grew 15 percent per year for the 2001–2002 period, and profits increased 20 percent for each of the two years.

Gillette continued to grow under Kilts's leadership. In 2005, the company was purchased by Procter & Gamble for $55 per share, almost double the price the stock had been when Kilts joined the troubled Gillette back in February 2001. When P&G took over Gillette, Kilts stayed for a brief period to help with the transition and then retired.

■ ■ ■

Hyundai and Gillette are powerful examples of what can happen when leaders adopt very clear visions, develop aggressive strategies, then drive those strategies to achieve the vision. So how can you achieve the same clarity of vision and strategy as that of the leaders at Hyundai and Gillette? Here are some key tips for developing strategies to make your vision a reality:

- *Assign the task to creative achievers.* You need to put somebody in charge to develop the specific strategies that will achieve the vision. You need to pick this person carefully. She should be an experienced individual who has continuously come up with bright ideas in the past and, most important, knows how to get results.

  As the leader, you need to make sure this individual realizes that her task must be a very interactive exercise with the organization. She needs to seek input broadly as to how the vision will be achieved. Throughout this process, she must step up and make decisions that will result in very clear, easy-to-understand strategies. It's also important that the person you select understands clearly that the exercise is of limited duration. You can't let a project drag on and on.

- *Make sure the proposed strategies achieve the vision.* As strategies are developed, what will often emerge is a variety of pet projects that people have wanted to pursue. You'll also hear some proposals aimed at minimizing the scope of change, so that employees can continue in their current role with only a few minor modifications. As a leader, you constantly need to challenge the various strategies that are being proposed to make sure that they actually do achieve the vision you have laid out. Jim Kilts of Gillette did this very well with his strong focus on getting firm commitments from his people regarding the impact of their strategies on revenue, profit, and market share.

- *Be tough on feasibility, cost, and timing.* As people sign up for positions of responsibility in executing the vision, you need to watch out for the natural tendency to build in all kinds of cushion with regard to cost and timing. You also need to push hard to make sure that what is being proposed is actually feasible. Often people will seize on some great new technology or some other faddish approach, only to find out later on that their assumptions were unrealistic.

One thing you must be careful of as a leader is not to be so intimidating that you push people into a plan that just can't be accomplished. Make it clear that you are honestly and objectively seeking the best strategies. You can't come across as a tough dictator who is simply barking out orders to be followed regardless of the implications.

The task of nailing down the strategies to achieve a vision should not be a painful one. Strong leaders make the process very interactive and fact driven, and it can become an engaging and exciting venture for the organization. This approach pays big dividends as you move to implementation.

## CAREFULLY SELECTED ACTIONABLE MEASURES

Once a leader has a vision and strategies in place, he or she has to institutionalize the means of meeting those goals. This is the time to reach for the old and reliable business adage: you get what you measure. Nothing beats a public report card. Courageous leaders establish measures of progress, publicize them, and act on the basis of the latest results. It is a leader's responsibility to take quick action when he or she first sees that measurable progress isn't happening. Beware of flawed measures; incorrect measurement of progress can lead to chaos, as demonstrated by the following example from the telecommunications industry.

Sprint and Nextel merged in December 2004 to great optimism and fanfare. Sprint was a long-distance provider famous for its striking ads about a fiber optic network so good you could "hear a pin drop." The cellular company Nextel was known for its "push to talk" technology and for having the best customer retention statistics of any telecom vendor in America. Now that Sprint Nextel was almost as big as the two giants in the industry, AT&T and Verizon Wireless, its executives believed that the company would have access to the latest technology from cell phone manufacturers and good prices on telecommunications equipment from the major vendors. Hence, with state-of-the-art phones, a competitive cost structure, and Nextel's industry-leading customer retention skills, Sprint Nextel would achieve its vision of effectively competing with AT&T and Verizon and become the wireless leader.

Soon after the merger in fall 2005, CEO Gary Forsee started talking up employees and the press about Sprint Nextel's vision of becoming the leader in wireless broadband services and content. Sprint's local telephone business would be spun off, partnerships with the cable industry formed, and a broadband wireless technology called WiMAX developed.[22] Unfortunately, Forsee didn't select the correct measures to achieve the vision. Cost cutting was his single-minded priority. He estimated synergies from the merger to be not the originally estimated $12 billion but $14.5 billion. Forsee's mixed message began to confuse not only Wall Street but also employees. It was not at all clear what the vision for the future really was, or what the key strategies were to achieve it. As one former executive told *Business Week*, "There was so much going on after the merger that there was a lack of focus."[23] Was the vision to be the wireless leader, based on great phones, superb cost management, and best-in-class customer retention? Or was it just to achieve the cost synergies and profits promised as part of the merger?

Shortly after the merger, it started to become clear that saving $14.5 billion purely through synergies was going to be, at best, tough. Forsee created huge pressure within Sprint Nextel to squeeze operations to make sure those aggressive financial projections would come true. The $14.5 billion became the vision, and cost cutting the strategy. Call centers started to be seen and measured mostly as cost centers, instead of as the pivotal tools for achieving industry-leading customer retention they should have been. Unfortunately, with the focus on cutting costs, customer service fell by the wayside.[24]

What was occurring was a serious mistake. No actionable measures were ever selected to achieve the original vision. Cost was the total focus. Nothing else mattered to the company. Given the original vision, there should have been actionable measures related to the competitiveness of its phones, customer service and retention, and cost.

One call center employee, Paula Pryor, said that the company became so strictly numbers-driven and cost-focused after the merger that "even bathroom trips were monitored. They would micro-manage us like children." Managers spent time monitoring how she used her computer. Overtime was cut back, and call center operators were urged to shorten their calls. The number of calls one could complete within an hour, she said, became the sole measure of performance.[25]

The primary customer service measure in the cell phone business is "churn," the percentage of your current customers who leave you each month. A former executive reported that whereas in the past the main focus at the board meetings had been churn, after the merger the focus quickly changed to cost management almost exclusively.[26] By late 2006, Sprint Nextel churn hit 2.4 percent, the highest in the telecommunications industry. Previously Nextel employees had taken pride in churn of 1.4 percent.

Another difficulty the company had was its slowness in merging systems. Customer service representatives had to access both the Sprint billing system and the Nextel billing system to answer customers' questions about their Sprint Nextel bills. One employee noted, "It was like Noah's Ark. We had two of everything."[27]

With plummeting customer satisfaction, high churn, and slow to no progress in achieving synergies in such areas as systems, the company came under severe financial pressure in 2006. In response, leaders put pressure on the call centers to have operators minimize the time spent with customers discussing their problems, and quickly get into a sales mode, pitching new Sprint Nextel services to those customers. The call centers were then given quotas for how many aggravated customers who wanted to cancel their accounts were strong-armed into extending their contracts and enrolling in new services. Employees could get bonuses ranging from $2,000 to $3,000 per month; naturally, "They wanted those big bonuses."[28] So customer satisfaction suffered, playing second fiddle to selling services incentivized by bonuses.

Soon the call centers were receiving complaints from customers that contracts were being extended without their approval, a practice that grew so pervasive that a class action suit was lodged. The attorney general of the State of Minnesota characterized Sprint Nextel as follows: "It's kind of like the Hotel California, where you can check in but never leave."[29]

Financial pressures continued to mount. In early 2007, to save money, the company began to cut back on the call center operators' ability to give customers favors like free phones and service credits. Neglect of customer satisfaction by management grew.

As you would expect, Sprint Nextel had real difficulty building a customer base with these new policies, and its churn remained high. In the third quarter of 2007, "Sprint subscriber numbers stayed flat at 54 million, while rivals AT&T and Verizon added millions." CEO Forsee was pressured by the board to step down in October 2007.[30]

During Forsee's reign at Sprint Nextel, the original vision and strategies were terrific, but he made a mistake by using cost savings as the only key measure. There were no measures used to drive excellence with regard to customer satisfaction with the phones and service or to market share. In January 2008, the company reported disastrous results from the last quarter of 2007, taking a merger-related charge of $30 billion that basically wiped out the deal's value. It also faced major lawsuits claiming that customer service contracts were being extended without people's agreement.

▦▦▦

Take the learning from this example to heart. After you select a vision and related strategies, be very careful in crafting the appropriate measures. Mistakes in this area can drive the organization in the wrong direction—away from achievement of the vision. The following are two very valuable points to remember:

1. *Measure the vision.* A leader needs to push hard to make sure that as measures are established, the job is getting done. Executing strategies well is important, but most important is achieving the

vision itself. If the strategies aren't creating the desired outcome, they aren't working. In our Sprint Nextel example, all the attention was on cost, as if cost excellence was the vision and cost cutting the strategy. The original vision was of growing market share versus AT&T and Verizon and becoming the wireless leader. The strategies were originally to have great phones, superb service, and an industry-leading cost structure. The primary measure should have been market share, while also measuring customer satisfaction with phones and service, retention, and cost. The selection of measures has big implications.

2. *Beware of flawed measures*. In setting up measures, you have to maintain a clear focus on what you truly want to achieve. Too often, companies develop measures that are handy but don't actually measure what they purport to, or don't address the underlying problem.

   I saw an example of a flawed measure recently. When a VP of sales at a major corporation wanted regular reports on a measure of customer satisfaction, the sales organization designed a survey to be sent out quarterly to a select group of customers. Unfortunately, the sales folks who selected the customers to be questioned picked those who they believed would be positive. Finally the VP got up the nerve to look into the matter and realized that he was being deceived because the measurement tool was flawed. The lesson is clear. A leader really needs to dig in and understand how any data offered as proof of progress have been put together, and what they really mean.

The cornerstone of an organization's success is a strong leader who has the courage to develop an exciting game plan consisting of a high-impact vision, clear strategies that will achieve it, and appropriate measures that will tell everyone whether or not the vision has been achieved. Don't forget that each step is as important as the others. Getting it right is hard work, but very rewarding.

# 3

## PRINCIPLE II

# Staff for Success

The more responsibility you bear as a leader, the more you realize how critically important talent is. You soon learn that you can't do everything yourself. You need to acquire the best talent possible, develop those individuals, and put them into the key assignments that are going to make a difference in achieving the vision and strategies of the organization. Over time, courageous leaders increasingly emphasize developing and properly utilizing the very best people. The situation within one consumer products company can shed light on just how important it is for a leader to come to grips with personnel issues and possess the ability to obtain quality information about performance in the organization.

The eastern regional sales manager of this company was a talented individual who had made rapid progress up the corporate ladder but was also having some very significant problems in his current assignment. His region was rated the lowest of the four U.S. regions in revenue growth over the previous twelve months, which was surprising. This individual had always risen to the occasion and was viewed as an absolute superstar within the company. He had been in the assignment for eighteen months at this juncture and was clearly struggling, given the disappointing revenue results.

His region had been struggling for years, which was the primary reason he had been put into the job eighteen months earlier. The company was confident that he could turn the situation around. However, he had two direct reports who were problematic. The district manager who had responsibility for Philadelphia had the worst numbers of all his direct reports. The Boston district manager was a close second. Unfortunately, there was no reliable performance appraisal system at the company, so the personnel files of both the Philadelphia and Boston district managers really didn't document any serious conversations about performance. HR sent forms out on an annual basis, but no one paid much attention to the process.

This eastern regional manager was thirty-five years old; the Philadelphia and Boston district managers were both between fifty-five and sixty. Both had been in their current assignments for well over ten years. The regional manager was told at the orientation for this role that these two individuals were extremely well regarded within sales and that their relationships with their customers were always viewed as exemplary. To make matters more complicated, the two problem district managers were close friends of the VP of sales. They were all about the same age and had all grown up in the company together.

The regional manager gathered as much data as possible on the sales results over the last five years for these two problematic managers. It turned out that they did very well with their food chain customers, but poorly with the drug chains and mass merchandisers in their areas. Going back ten to fifteen years, most of this consumer product company's sales were to food chains. During the last ten years, drug chains and mass merchandisers had become the major growth channels.

The regional manager took a month to visit with some of the sales reps in those two districts to learn how they were feeling about the business and about their district sales managers. What he found out was that there was significant de-emphasis of anything but food chains, and although any bright ideas on how to stimulate the drug and mass merchandiser business were received graciously, nothing was ever done. The conclusion was very clear. These two district managers hadn't grown with the company and weren't doing anything differently than they had fifteen years earlier. They also had been receiving no feedback about their weak performance over the years. The troops clearly saw the problem and were frustrated by the fact that management had done little about it.

Fortunately, the remedies were also clear. The eastern regional manager had to confront the VP of sales with the unsatisfactory performance of these two individuals and immediately move them out. Also, HR needed to be confronted about the inadequate performance appraisal process, as that department was the reason for the lack of quality performance data on people in the company. Given the weakness of the two individuals' businesses, and the strength and thoroughness of the regional manager's analysis and recommendations provided to the VP of sales, the eastern region was given the OK to move into action to clean things up.

␣␣␣

Unfortunately, this sort of situation is quite typical. Leaders don't like to confront poor performance and, rather than address the situation, will often just leave people in jobs they are doing inadequately. Also, performance appraisal processes can atrophy quickly, and over time the organization loses its ability to deal with personnel issues or develop talent.

The rest of this chapter outlines some valuable guidelines that, if followed, will enable you to match the right people with the right jobs and to move quickly to exploit opportunities and put the most talented individuals into place to turn those opportunities into success.

# PERFORM RIGOROUS PERFORMANCE ASSESSMENTS

Nothing hurts morale and an organization's bottom line as much as weak talent and underutilization of exceptional performers. Yet many organizations fail to make this issue a priority. Here I will highlight why this topic is so important and describe how a first-rate performance appraisal system can help. We will then discuss the basic—and essential—components of your appraisal system.

## The Why

No matter whether you are a company, a nonprofit, a governmental organization, or an educational institution, allowing poor performers to continue to struggle and failing to aggressively identify and stretch your very strong performers generate two very significant problems:

1. *Endorsing mediocrity.* When you allow weak performers to continue to plod along, your organization is not performing as it should. Even worse, often you reach a point where you know that the individual can't be productive, but you avoid confronting the issue, giving him meaningless activities and simply ignoring him. You are wasting money, you are wasting that individual's time, and the organization is not facing the reality of the situation. You are also irritating a number of other employees in the organization who have to work with this individual. Most important, you are discouraging the strong performers who see this kind of thing going on and often conclude that endorsing mediocrity is not for them and that they don't want to be part of the organization.

2. *Underutilizing talent.* Failing to identify your strong performers and stretch them by putting them in key assignments deprives you of the opportunity to benefit from their good ideas, their drive for progress, and the results they can achieve for the organization. Equally unfortunate, they may become bored and leave. Strong performers need to be told they are strong, and they need to be further developed. Your organization will then have a growing pool of high-potential personnel to tackle your toughest challenges—and yield better results.

A good performance appraisal system prevents both of these problems. By focusing on improving the performance of every employee, an effective system enables you to directly confront the problems some individuals may be having and to develop your very best people very quickly.

Incredible things can happen when you put your strong performers against specific and stretching goals. Steve Jobs of Apple knows this. Back in 2000, he spotted the unique skills of Tony Fadell, a very experienced and talented hardware designer. Jobs hired Fadell and had him lead a very small and secret team with the objective of coming up with a device that would take advantage of digital media and provide individual consumers with a revolutionary portable music device. Fadell and his small team developed the iPod, launched in fall 2001, which has both invigorated and revolutionized Apple as a company and turned the music industry on its head.

Back in 1993, the chairman of Toyota selected Yoshiro Kimbara, a very talented executive with years of exceptional results at Toyota, and asked him to think about what car Toyota should be designing for a world in which oil prices would be a lot higher and the environment more of a concern. Kimbara came back suggesting they build a hybrid car as an experiment and see whether or not it made sense. The resulting Prius was launched in 1997 and has been an incredible leadership product for Toyota and for the entire automobile business.

You need to stretch your strong performers and create an environment where they love to work. Typically, they don't like an environment loaded up with mediocre and poorly performing individuals who drag down the quality of their own work, nor one in which they are not challenged. This is yet another argument for an effective performance appraisal system that allows you to regularly evaluate the performance of all employees and focus on improving their contribution.

## The How

Over my forty years of business experience, I've seen a couple of really good performance appraisal systems, and I've seen a whole lot more that are below average to poor. The one with which I was most impressed was the appraisal system in use at Microsoft from 1994 to 2001 during my years as COO. Bill Gates designed this system when the company was very small, and he was a very strong proponent of it year after year. It was clear to me that it paid big dividends for Microsoft.

How did the Microsoft system work? It was a five-point system; let's call the scores one to five, although that is not exactly what was used. If you were a manager who had over a hundred or so employees under your supervision, the annual performance ratings you gave to each of your employees every August had to fit into the following five-point distribution:

*The five rating.* These were the genuine stars, and across your population of personnel, 10 percent of your employees had to be given this rating. You could make an exception and award the rating to 11 percent or 9 percent, but the goal was 10 percent. (Clearly the 10 percent was a bit arbitrary, as were the percentages for the other ratings explained here, but there had to be a target so that the managers were required to carefully sort out the relative performance of their employees.)

*The four rating.* These individuals were above-average performers who were not quite as good as your "fives," but they were very talented. Across your population, you had to award this rating to very close to 20 percent of your employees.

*The three rating.* Although these employees were average, they were quite valuable to the company. You gave this rating to 50 percent of your employees; you could vary that number by 1 or 2 percentage points, but that's all.

*The two rating.* These individuals had clear areas of improvement that needed to be tackled. Their performance would be classified as below average, and if they deteriorated further, there would be big problems. You had to give this rating to 15 percent of your employees.

*The one rating.* These individuals were seriously lagging behind their peers in performance. For each of them, a three- to six-month program was put in place to achieve very significant improvement. If they did not improve, they would be given three to six months to find employment outside the company that would fit them better. You had to give this rating to 5 percent of your employees.

During the performance review, the manager discussed the employee's rating, his or her strengths and weaknesses, and why the employee received the particular rating. Managers wrote up thorough analyses of performance, and in each case, both the supervisor and the subordinate were required to sign that write-up. It was then submitted to HR. For a particular department, if HR did not have all the completed and signed performance appraisals in hand by the target date, none of the individuals in that department would receive their salary increases. As you would expect, this meant that 100 percent of the performance appraisals would be completed on time!

The salary increases that went along with the performance reviews varied quite significantly in size. For example, if the overall salary increase that year was 5 percent, the fives might receive an 11 to 12 percent increase; the fours might get a 8 or 9 percent increase, the threes a 4 percent increase, and the twos a 1 or 2 percent increase. Those with a rating of one wouldn't get any salary increase. In far too many organizations, the strong and the weak performers all receive salary increases of about the same size. That sends a terrible message to strong performers.

The Microsoft system did an excellent job of making sure that individuals knew where they stood, which benefited both the employees and the company. The employees rated five were typically selected for the most important assignments in order to develop them further and to achieve great performance against the key tasks within the company. The one- and two-rated employees were dealt with appropriately.

The key point here is not that you need to duplicate the Microsoft system but that you do need a disciplined, standardized system in which everyone is reviewed, the top 10 to 15 percent are identified and stretched, and the bottom 5 to 7 percent are required to improve or be fired or moved to a more suitable job within the company. If you don't at least capture these two ends of the bell-shaped curve and instead allow managers to rate employees at their discretion, I can guarantee you that all ratings will be inflated, and rarely will poor performers be dealt with properly.

The kind of system I am recommending yields huge benefits for the company. Individuals are dealt with honestly, progress on key projects improves, and overall organizational performance is enhanced.

## The Typical Approach

In many organizations, once a year HR will pass out performance review guidelines and forms, indicating that it is now time for that annual exercise, along with a target date for completion. In my consulting work, I've often found that HR is really not disciplined about this task. HR people don't require that the forms be signed by both parties and collected by HR. In fact, in many cases, the performance appraisals simply never happen.

The reason why they don't happen is that it's hard to give a performance appraisal. No one wants to do it. The supervisor doesn't want to do it because it is uncomfortable and feels unnatural to describe the shortcomings of other individuals. Subordinates don't want their performance appraised, because even if they are strong performers, the boss will find something to complain about. If they are average-to-weak performers, it's no fun to sit there and have their boss dwell on their problems and shortcomings. The typical attitude of both the subordinate and the supervisor is, Let's just ignore the whole thing. That's why in most cases, performance appraisals never happen. This means that the company is giving lower priority to developing talent and putting less emphasis on achieving business goals, both of which should be unacceptable to a strong leader.

## The Basic Requirements

Every organization needs a rigorous performance appraisal system. But how should such a system be structured? The important question to ask is, "What are the basic requirements that any performance appraisal system ought to have?" This is an important issue, as there are a lot of different ways to approach the performance assessment process. Here is what I believe are the fundamental components:

- *Isolate the top 10 percent.* The most important aspect of a performance appraisal system is spotting your really strong performers and stretching them appropriately. They represent the future of your organization, and you need to invest in them heavily. Most important, this means you must have a high-quality approach to finding these people in the first place.
- *Isolate the bottom 5 to 7 percent.* If performance excellence is a goal, it's critical to constantly isolate people who simply aren't able to make the grade. Every year you should clearly identify the 5 to 7 percent of your organization who don't perform as well as the other 93 to 95 percent. The recruiting process can never be perfect, so you are always going to end up with a spectrum of people from super-strong performers to the very weak. To continually strive for excellence means you have to confront the fact that there will be some weak performers, and you need either to let them go or to find a job for them that is a better fit.
- *Match rewards to performance.* If the average salary increase is going to be 5 percent, your top performers should get at least twice that. Your weak performers should receive virtually no increase. Too often you see organizations where differences in salary increases between the top and bottom performers are quite narrow. That's simply wrong. Your dollars need to match your words to employees concerning their performance.
- *Calibrate the middle.* As I discussed earlier, Microsoft broke those who were not in the top or bottom groups into three parts: the two, three, or four ratings. It's not critical to break this middle group into three pieces. What is important is to have some kind of calibration process so that you know which groups of people are

clearly high performers and low performers. Personally, I think that not breaking up the middle 80 percent or so into smaller groups is a missed opportunity. Breaking this group down allows you to make valid distinctions among that big group, to acknowledge and motivate the strongest and to warn the weakest of their need for improvement. However, I've seen some organizations appraise this group as one and simply charge the managers to discuss strengths and weaknesses, encourage improvement where needed, and praise good work.

- *Make the system foolproof.* Nothing atrophies like a performance assessment system. As I noted earlier, nobody wants to have a performance appraisal, neither subordinates nor supervisors. This is why you need a rigorous, foolproof system that requires everyone to go through this tough exercise, document it, and have it recorded by your HR department. Whatever system you develop, it's vitally important that it be foolproof. Performance appraisals must take place, and they must be documented. The person being evaluated needs to sign a summary of it, indicating that he or she has received the appraisal and the rating. Anything short of that and I can guarantee you that within two or three years, half your people won't be receiving performance appraisals.

- *Ensure regular timing.* Employees who have been with the organization less than five years should be assessed every six months so that they know what kind of progress they are making as they become more and more acclimated to the company. After five years, an annual assessment is probably all that is necessary.

In any organization, achieving great results is totally dependent on having great talent. The only way to nurture great talent is to deal with performance very objectively and concretely. The business world has proven over and over that this is hard to do, and that if you are to successfully grow the people who will enable you to grow the impact of your organization, you need a disciplined, standardized system that is well executed by HR.

# MOVE WEAK PERFORMERS OUT QUICKLY

One of the most common mistakes made in industry is to leave mediocre performers in their jobs way too long. It is difficult to confront poor performance. There is no doubt about that. It's one of the toughest things that a manager has to do. Nevertheless, you have to realize that you are facing big risks by not dealing with the situation. Those risks are as follows:

- *Hurting the culture.* When you have a mediocre performer leading a group of people, the individuals who work for that person know there is a problem. Also, when an individual contributor, not a manager of people, is not performing well, his or her peers know it. By not dealing with such situations, you are indicating that this is a nonconfrontational culture that allows poor performance or bad behavior. Very simply, people can get away with things. It sends a clear message that people don't have to work that hard around here.
- *Hurting the group's impact.* By leaving a poor performer in place, you are a contributor to subpar performance for that unit. You can blame it on the weak performer, but the fact is, you are just as responsible as anyone for putting up with less than stellar results.
- *Creating opportunities for competitors.* By having employees who don't jump on new ideas or perform the basic business in the best possible way, you open up opportunities for your competitors. Once again, you can't blame anyone but yourself when your competitor beats you to the marketplace with an idea or outperforms you with respect to a particular aspect of the business.

Let's take a look at a company that exhibited poor personnel management and so had some of these problems within the organization. This example shows the problems that result from being unwilling to move people out as soon as they start showing themselves to be weak performers. Although this particular case describes a problem at the CEO level, the same principles apply to all levels within a company.

Digital Equipment Corporation (DEC) pressured IBM intensely with its sensational VAX minicomputers, which peaked in popularity in the late 1980s. The minicomputer was truly a revolutionary product in the computer industry in that, at last, there was an alternative to the mainframe that IBM dominated. DEC was founded by Ken Olsen, who served as the CEO throughout the 1980s and early 1990s. Olsen was even named *Fortune* magazine's "America's Most Successful Entrepreneur" in 1986 for his role in bringing the minicomputer to the market.

But Olsen fell too much in love with the minicomputer. He scoffed at personal computers as well as desktop workstations when they came on strong in the late 1980s, and it was Olsen's decision not to have DEC develop such products. Celebrated throughout the 1980s as an incredible innovator, Olsen perennially appeared on business magazine covers. In the process, so seduced by his own success, he'd become blind to new technologies.

In the late 1980s, the workstation, offering radically increased power at much lower cost, began to supersede the minicomputer, just as minis had done to the low-end mainframes of the 1970s. DEC's core problem in the late 1980s and early 1990s was that "instead of rushing to offer competitive workstations, the company initially responded with scorn, losing billions of dollars of potential orders from such loyal customers as Boeing and National Semiconductor," according to *Fortune*.[1]

Olsen received a fair amount of criticism during this period of the early 1990s. For example, Gordon Bell, the head of engineering for DEC and the leader of the VAX development team, was driven out by Olsen because he thought Olsen was out of touch with the industry; when Bell was asked by *Fortune* about DEC being out of touch, he commented, "Olsen is their number one problem."[2]

Surprisingly, DEC's board of directors continued to support Olsen, and in April 1992 the company reported a quarterly profit loss of $294 million.[3] Things soon got worse as the minicomputer market basically disappeared, with workstations and PCs taking their place. This caused

DEC to lay off twenty thousand people, generating a huge write-off and a staggering loss of $2.8 billion.[4]

Given that the DEC product line was out-of-date and the company was losing big money ($251 million in 1993), in July 1993 the board of directors finally made its move and forced Olsen out of the CEO job. The question is, why did they wait so long? They should have acted immediately when Olsen was making statements in the late 1980s about workstations being toys compared to the DEC minicomputer line.[5]

Although new leadership tried to resuscitate DEC, their efforts failed. The company was eventually sold to Compaq, and the only component that was retained by Compaq to generate revenue was the services arm. It's a sad tale of a company failing simply because the board waited too long to replace a leader who clearly had become incapable of innovating in a way that would have enabled the company to compete in the fast-paced computer industry.

These same kinds of issues come up over and over again in companies at all levels, but can be easily avoided by nipping poor performance in the bud when it starts. Here are some simple guidelines to follow on an ongoing basis to avoid these kinds of problems:

- *Implement high-quality performance appraisals.* As mentioned previously, you need a system that regularly and clearly makes every member of your organization aware of his or her strengths and weaknesses and how his or her overall performance is regarded. Only by having a track record over the months and years will you be able to defend any decision you may make in the future to move poor performers out.
- *Give early warnings.* You have to confront weak performance as soon as you detect it and make it clear to the individual that things have to change. Too often, we see examples of the boss who never talks to the subordinate about his or her poor performance and then, after a lengthy period, a crisis emerges. The boss wants to

get rid of the individual for performance reasons. This can lead to legal problems if in fact you haven't been discussing performance issues on a regular basis. Thousands of lawsuits are initiated every year by individuals who believe they were released without due cause. The real problem was that the boss was afraid to warn the individual about the poor performance but finally got fed up with it. This was clearly the case with DEC; the board of directors should have started raising issues in the mid-to-late 1980s as PCs and workstations emerged.

- *Strengthen the talent pool.* You need to be constantly developing talent so that when you do make changes, you'll have people ready to take on the new responsibilities. It can be devastating to face a crucial need, yet just not have the talent required to rise to the occasion. Stretching and challenging your best people prepares them for crucial needs when they emerge.

- *Move people around regularly.* After two or three years, people can become stale in a job. Also, they have probably learned just about all they are going to learn. Hence, it is usually a good idea to move them to a new assignment. This is particularly true for your strong performers. By moving them around, you can further develop their skills and benefit from their prior experiences.

Remember, don't wait long to get rid of weak performers. You have to fight off all those human tendencies to accept the status quo, and deal with the situation. Hesitation can have serious consequences for the entire organization.

## USE EMPLOYEE SURVEYS TO SPOT WEAK PERFORMANCE

One key way to spot underperforming leaders in an organization is to make smart use of annual or semiannual employee surveys. In many companies, this tool is vastly underutilized. Too often, it is not really taken seriously and so falls into disrepair. In my experiences at Microsoft, Procter & Gamble, and the many other companies for whom I have consulted, I've found only a few companies that both executed a well-designed employee survey with excellence and used the data effectively—for example, by breaking that data out by department head and vice president so as to evaluate manager performance.

Let's start from the beginning and analyze why it is appropriate to conduct a regular employee survey. The following benefits can do wonders in early detection of some key problems:

- *Taking the temperature of the troops.* A well-executed employee survey enables the leaders of the company to gain a concrete understanding of how things are going among the workforce; for example, Are employees getting regular feedback from their boss? Have they had a formal performance appraisal in the past year? Is the company heading in the right direction? Is their department's strategy clear? and so on. Without this kind of formalized tool that generates objective data, you are simply operating on the basis of anecdotes and possibly misleading complaints. There is simply no substitute for a well-designed employee survey that generates quantitative measures (typically on a 5-point scale, with the midpoint representing neutral) of a variety of different aspects of an organization's performance. To give you an example: I did some work for one company where the CEO was convinced he had clearly and regularly reminded the employees of the game plan for the next two years, but 68 percent of employees disagreed (gave scores of 2 or 1 on the 5-point scale) with the survey statement "I am aware of and understand the company's strategy for the next two years."

- *Spotting weak departments and leaders.* Although you want the survey to be anonymous, the employees should be asked to indicate the department and division in which they are working—but only if the organization is large enough that it won't be obvious which employee is associated with which completed questionnaire. The resulting information can then be broken down by vice president or by department head so that you can see what each leader's group is thinking and feeling. It is likely you will see clear differences in the employee groups, and often these differences will point to the leadership abilities or deficiencies of the person in charge.

- *Spotting communication gaps.* By having employees comment on the clarity of their goals and the clarity of the overall goals of the company, you can gain good insight into what leaders are communicating to their employees. Are the leaders of various units correctly communicating to their teams what the company as a whole is trying to do, and setting goals to meet that vision?

- *Spotting emerging turnover problems.* By including questions designed to measure employees' overall satisfaction with their jobs, such as whether or not an employee believes that he or she will be working for the company in two to three years, you can gain good insight into emerging turnover problems.

Naturally, tracking trends on these measures year by year is the key to understanding movement in some of these important statistics.

### The Basics of a Good Survey

Every company should design a survey of its own that captures some of the characteristics of its industry, the way the company is organized, and any other issues that are uniquely important. Regardless of your company's industry or unique characteristics, however, there are seven basic categories that ought to be included. For each of the following seven categories, I provide two to four statements that will help you gauge the state of things within your company. For each of these statements, my experience is that a simple 5-point scale works best. Specifically, you ask the employee to read each statement and then rate it as follows: strongly agree (5), agree (4), neutral (3), disagree (2), or strongly disagree (1). Although you may want to word the questions differently depending on the nature of your organization, it's important to cover these basics.

1. Your Job

    My responsibilities are clear.

    I have the authority to carry out the responsibility assigned to me.

    I like my job.

    When I do very good work, it is recognized.

2. Your Boss

    I have confidence in my boss.

    My boss provides clear goals for me to work toward.

    I get helpful feedback from my boss on a regular basis.

3. Your Development

    During the past year, I have significantly enhanced my skills.

    I see lots of opportunities for me to grow at this company.

    My manager has a sincere interest in my career.

4. Your Group/Peers

    My work group works toward clear goals.

    There is good cooperation between my work group and other
        groups.

5. Your Compensation

    My salary is fair and competitive.

    My total compensation is fair and competitive.

    The company has good benefits.

6. The Company Strategy and Leaders

    I believe the company is headed in the right direction.

    I get regular updates on the direction of the company and how it
        is doing.

    I have confidence in the leadership of the VP of my division.

7. Longevity

    I feel respected and valued.

    Working for this company is a good deal.

    I will probably be working for this company three years
        from now.

Once again, although these questions isolate the basics and would provide excellent fundamental information on the health of the organization, you may wish to add other questions on specific aspects of your organization's performance that you want to measure. Many employee surveys end up with fifty or sixty different categories, but what you have to keep in mind is that you want the employee to be able to complete the survey in a reasonable amount of time. Long surveys can be dangerous because the individual becomes impatient with the process. Hence, as with most things in life, brevity is highly valued.

**Ensuring Quality Execution**

Here are a few tips for managing the employee survey to make sure it's executed regularly and well. Again, experience suggests that it is very easy to let the employee survey process atrophy over time. It requires strong executive leadership to make sure the following points get higher priority:

- *Give one person responsibility.* It's best to put one senior HR person in charge of the employee survey project. That individual should be held accountable not only for conducting the survey well but for summarizing the key findings from it and making sure that the organization is utilizing its results.
- *Freeze the wording of questions.* It is important to phrase the survey questions with care. There should be no ambiguity. For anyone reading a question, the intent should be crystal clear. Most important, once wording is decided on, it should not be changed from year to year. Changing the wording can significantly change the way a question is interpreted, so the resulting data will not be comparable from year to year. If you change the wording, your ability to observe trends over time will be spoiled. Market research professionals know this well, and you should have whoever is in charge of your employee survey make sure that he or she is tapping some market research expertise in putting the survey together and in maintaining it year to year. (There is no problem with adding a few questions each year

that address particular issues, but you should not add a lot, or you are changing the nature of the survey.)

- *Aim for 100 percent participation.* You must find a way to guarantee participation, but because it is critical that you receive open and frank responses, you also need to assure employees that their responses will remain anonymous. Here, information technology can help, allowing surveys to be submitted so that the system will know if the survey has been completed, while keeping the identity of the individual's response entirely confidential. Your employees need to be satisfied that their identity is being totally protected.

### Reporting the Results

The person responsible for fielding and executing the survey should also be responsible for making sure that an overall report summarizing the results is generated. The report should also break out the data by division VP and by department head. This allows individual departments to understand how their people responded and, most important, how those responses are different from those of other divisions or other departments or the overall corporate result. Experience suggests that it's best for the individual divisions and departments to summarize the data in terms of findings, conclusions, and action steps, because doing so enables them to reflect on their recent practices and what may or may not be working. At the same time, the management of the company needs to show real interest in seeing those reports broken out by division and department head.

The real value in this survey is in calibrating departments and divisions and spotting trends over the years for the whole company. For example, suppose that for four years, 70 percent of employees in a particular division agreed or strongly agreed with the statement "My salary is fair and competitive," but then over the next two years, that figure dropped to 58 percent and then to 41 percent, while other divisions remained stable at around 65 percent on this attribute. Clearly it is time to ask the division VP what is going on in the salary area. The HR organization needs to play a strong role here in making sure the data are summarized properly, that they get attention, and that the organization capitalizes on what is learned. The examples that follow show what important information two organizations uncovered by making very good use of their employee surveys.

### Uncovering a Lack of Vision

I once spent time consulting with a company that had historically been very successful; in the three years prior to my consultation, however, the business was basically flat, and, more important, the turnover of personnel had significantly increased. This organization had regularly administered an employee survey, but had given it virtually no visibility. In fact, the leadership of the organization viewed the employee survey merely as something that HR did once a year, and they paid no attention to it.

In working with the HR personnel responsible for the survey, I asked to look at the last five years of data. Although the survey wasn't perfect and some of the questions had had their wording changed a few times, there were a set of key questions that had remained the same, so some trends could be reliably tracked.

One of the questions was worded as follows: "I understand the company's business strategy and think it will work." Over the last five years, the percentage of employees who strongly agreed or agreed with that statement showed the following declining trend: 72, 74, 65, 58, 61. In response, the CEO had HR interview people about their confidence in the company's direction. What they learned was that the employees were proud of the company and the strong performance it had achieved, but there was a general sense of "Where do we go from here?" There was no uniform awareness of what the company was trying to achieve or what the near-term goals were.

It became clear as I worked with the management team that the employees were correct. The company's historical success had led the management to grow complacent, and they really didn't have a clear vision designed to move the business ahead. This wasn't a matter of managers' failing to communicate company goals to the employees;

management simply lacked a strategic plan for the future. Although the employee survey didn't uncover this problem directly, it supplied a big clue. Taking an objective reading of the employee base and properly analyzing the results can yield valuable information. In this case, that information caused management to get serious about developing an aggressive strategic plan. The organization also began placing much higher priority on the employee survey, with higher-quality personnel in charge of it.

**Uncovering Weakness in Management**

One company I worked with provides a really strong example of how valuable an employee survey can be in spotting a key manager's weakness, confronting the problem, and getting it fixed. In this case, the individual was one of eighteen vice presidents and also a division manager of one of the nine operating divisions for this particular company.

For the annual employee survey, each respondent designated which VP he or she worked for. The HR organization then broke out the survey results by VP. Each VP got to see, for the various questions, how his or her employees responded. The VPs also got to see overall, and for each particular attribute, how they ranked in comparison to the other seventeen VPs. This is powerful.

The particular VP with whom I was working was rated quite low on the following question: "I have confidence in the leadership of the VP of my division." Of the eighteen vice presidents, he was second from the bottom. He couldn't see the names of the other seventeen VPs; he just knew that there was one who ranked lower than he and sixteen who ranked higher.

This VP also rated low on the question "I understand the goals and objectives of my division." On this question, the VP scored sixteenth. Again, he didn't know the names of the other VPs and their ratings; he simply knew where he ranked.

For this VP, the results were shocking and embarrassing. He was relatively new to the job, having been promoted to the vice presidential level only fifteen months before. Over the years, he had been a very strong performer in the company, but this was his first job managing a very big group—well over seven hundred people. In his prior jobs, he had never managed more than a hundred. Regardless, the learning from the survey was very clear, and he knew what he had to do. He needed to create a device that regularly told the troops what the organization was trying to accomplish and what its game plan was. Also, I encouraged him to create a quarterly report telling all the employees in his division how things were going and what the immediate challenges were.

The VP reported to the president of the company, who was well aware of the ratings of all the VPs, so of course this topic of inadequate communication instantly became an item of discussion between the VP and his boss. But most important, the VP tackled his weakness with gusto, and two years later was promoted to group VP.

Without the survey, it would have been hard to detect this gap in communication, which was clearly impairing the effectiveness of that VP and of his organization. The lesson is clear. Development of your key leaders can be greatly enhanced by properly executing an employee survey and then breaking out the results so that you can spot any weaknesses in your up-and-coming leaders. This will make sure that they are learning and growing as quickly as possible.

An employee survey can be a great aid in developing personnel and understanding key workforce issues. But beware: a survey requires some real quality attention and ownership to make it work hard for you.

I cannot emphasize enough how important your staff is. You must put a very high priority on getting the right people in the key jobs, dealing with weak performance quickly, and having great tools like a good performance appraisal system and a high-quality employee survey procedure to keep your talent pool strong. A strong leader knows that talent makes all the difference.

# 4

## PRINCIPLE III

# Clean Up the Sloppiness

I'm quite sure that most people have experienced the frustration of having roadblock after roadblock thrown up in front of them as they tried to get something accomplished. They reach the point where they realize that the world just can't be that complex. When easy things are hard to do, it's an obvious sign that it's time to clean up the organization and get back to the simple world we all love to operate in. Typically, complexity and sloppiness in a company are due to excessive headcount, fragmented and independent organizations, lack of standardized practices, and disjointed and antiquated information systems. The tough part for a manager is getting up the courage to tackle these problems, knowing full well that many people will feel the impact or even be eliminated.

I once worked with a company that had suffered badly in the marketplace for two or three years. The core problem was that it just couldn't get its innovative ideas into the marketplace in a timely manner. Also, just to operate day in and day out within the company was painful. I conducted interviews with middle managers, and they consistently cited their frustration with getting even the simplest things accomplished.

Another problem they were having, which was viewed as even more serious, was very high turnover of personnel in the middle-manager ranks, particularly among the top performers at those levels. The leaders had no idea whether the turnover problem was related to the complexity issue or something else. I was brought in as a consultant, and asked to do some interviews to investigate. After initial discussions with the top management, we decided I would first focus on the turnover issue.

This organization had five product divisions that operated quite independently. On the basis of my limited number of interviews in these divisions, it was not clear if all five divisions were experiencing this middle-level manager turnover problem or whether it was related to a particular division or two. Also, I sensed that salary increases were being implemented such that really strong performers were given roughly the same percentage increase in salary as the weak performers; more important, larger increases were being given to the higher-level people, and middle- and lower-level managers were being given very modest increases.

The obvious next step was to look at the salary data. The CEO of the company was very interested in this turnover issue and pulled together the VPs of the five product divisions as well as the VP of HR to find out what the facts were regarding turnover. One task was to break down the turnover rate by division and by level, and to break down salary increase percentages by division, level, and performance rating. Another was to find out whether or not most of the incremental salary dollars were going to the high-level jobs, shortchanging middle-level management and lower-level employees, and to discover if the strong performers were being rewarded significantly better than the average and weak performers.

The HR VP explained that we would need to get IT involved because much of the data required for that kind of analysis resided in a variety of different databases throughout the operating divisions, and each division designed its own databases and data definitions. Embarrassingly, the HR VP also explained that performance appraisal data were unreliable in most of the databases and that in many cases, they were not even entered into a database. For a couple of the divisions, there weren't even up-to-date databases, so investigating whether the different levels of management were being treated differently was going to be very hard to do.

A few weeks after this session, the CEO was told that the IT organization would have to launch a major effort that would take about six months and cost just short of $500,000 to pull together the necessary data from these various operating divisions. The CEO was also told that in many cases, the data simply did not exist, so there would be holes in the analysis.

The complexity and frustration associated with trying to get this basic data were ridiculous. All kinds of systems, databases, and processes were in place, but they were totally fragmented, incompatible, and sloppily maintained, because no one was in control.

Unfortunately, many organizations play out this kind of scenario as they mature. Even though such core processes as salary management, performance management, and the tracking of headcount and turnover are basic, they become fragmented and complicated beyond belief. This causes organizations to end up flying blind: they lack a basic understanding of what is happening internally. They can't even get to the data. A company should define the basic HR data, finance data, and so on in one way across the entire company and have basic systems and databases that enable thorough analysis of what is happening in the company and in the various divisions.

In the case of the company with which I was consulting, the CEO made the tough decision to replace the VPs of HR and IT, as they were clearly ineffectual. Then the CEO had to make sure the new VPs understood the need for corporate standards and draconian simplicity.

▨ ▨ ▨

Another company I worked with was an example of how organizations can become complex and slow due to excessive layers of management. I was doing some work with a consumer products company that was falling badly behind their competition and losing market share in many of their categories. In talking to the brand management personnel at this company, I discovered that they were extremely frustrated with how hard it was to get work done, and the frustration was primarily related to the number of levels of approval they had to struggle through before a new idea could be put in the marketplace.

One brand manager in the health and beauty aid area of the business described an experience he had when a new package was being developed for one of their shampoo brands. There was tremendous excitement about coupling that new package with a modest formula and fragrance change that would improve the appeal of this shampoo. When the brand group got to the point where they were ready to test-market the product, they had to get the approval of the associate marketing manager, then the marketing manager of the division, then the division VP. Getting each of these approvals took weeks, due to difficulty scheduling meetings and then having to answer questions and modify their proposal to reflect comments.

Having gotten all of those folks on board, the division VP then decided he should also get the OK of his boss, a group VP of the company whose background was mostly manufacturing. Unfortunately, after reading the proposal, the group VP complained that he did not think they needed to change the bottle shape because it would require the manufacturing plant to retool the production lines to fit this new bottle. He was not aware that the manufacturing folks had already agreed to the change and considered it no big deal. This intervention by the group VP generated three weeks of e-mail exchanges, meetings, and documents laying out the facts until finally that executive agreed.

Unfortunately, once the bottle issue was resolved, the group VP then brought up another. He had been talking with the VP of procurement about using this bottle change as an opportunity to scale back from four bottle suppliers to three. This set off a two-week debate because the lower-level procurement people had already reviewed that issue and told the brand group that they wanted to stay with the four. The VP of procurement had agreed with his people, but to help the group VP save face, he suggested to the group VP that it would probably be best to get the test-market started, and if it was determined that the test-market was going to be expanded nationally, procurement would revisit the vendor issue then.

Clearly this company was top heavy!

I'm sure all of us have experienced this sense of frustration when we have to work with numerous layers of management that don't share our sense of urgency to get to the marketplace as quickly as possible with a bright idea. To help avoid such waste, a leader needs to constantly strive for simplicity regarding how work is done.

The remainder of this chapter focuses on three very straightforward guidelines that every organization, be it large or small, needs to follow to keep things simple so that it's better able to compete.

## MINIMAL SYSTEMS AND PROCESSES

A key task of any leader is to keep systems and processes very simple and headcount low. Experience suggests that this is quite hard to do. Virtually every day you read about some company needing to lay off thousands. The tendency to get fat and slow is very real. Excess personnel and complicated and fragmented processes and systems cause things to move at a snail's pace. It requires a lot of courage for leaders to constantly say no to any attempt to complicate how work gets done.

Hewlett-Packard is a perfect example of a company that let its systems and processes get so overly complicated that it was unable to properly analyze how the business was doing. Luckily, in 2005 Mark Hurd, the relatively new CEO of HP, had the vision to bring in talent that could turn things around.

When Hurd convinced Randy Mott to join the company as the chief information officer, the systems and processes within the company could hardly have been more of a mess. The IT organization consisted of nineteen thousand people, about six thousand computer application programs that were used to run the company, and eighty-five different data centers. HP was spending about 5 percent of revenue on IT.[1] Hurd wanted that to go down to 2 percent, putting HP in a strong competitive position in the IT industry. The IT staff was scattered throughout the globe, residing in more than a hundred different HP locations.[2]

Mott had spent twenty-two years in IT at Walmart and was very well respected in the IT industry. His claim to fame at Walmart was building one gigantic data warehouse on which Walmart relied heavily to analyze consumer purchase trends and to coordinate the world-class logistics procedures that kept Walmart shelves stocked nearly all day, every day.[3] Sam Walton hated an out-of-stock situation, so he learned to love Mott's systems. Mott left Walmart in 2000 to join Dell, where he developed a single data warehouse to assist Dell in coordinating raw material orders from its suppliers to facilitate Dell's "build to order" just-in-time production approach.[4]

When Mott was launching the data warehousing efforts at both Walmart and Dell, Hurd was the CEO at NCR Corporation. NCR supplied the massive data management equipment required to build the data warehouses Mott was assembling at the time, so Mott was Hurd's customer. Because Hurd was aware of Mott's successes at Walmart and Dell, it didn't take him long after becoming CEO at HP to seek out Mott and hire him to clean up HP's enormous mess.

Soon after Mott arrived at HP, he and Hurd quickly agreed on their IT dream of a huge data warehouse that would enable HP, for the first time, to know what a specific customer was buying from all the different divisions of HP. Knowing the total picture for a particular customer would enable the HP sales organizations to take advantage of the tremendous breadth of the HP product line and sell more products to each customer.

At the time, all the key customer data were fragmented in the almost eight hundred databases sprinkled around the company at its eighty-five different data centers. There was almost no way to know the full scope of what a particular customer was buying from HP. A particular division knew what it was selling to a customer, but there was no way to gauge the overall impact that HP, as a company, was having on that customer. Also, it was nearly impossible to take a particular geographic area in the world and understand how well HP was doing cumulatively across all its product lines in that area. At the time, Hurd commented, "We shipped 55 million printers, 30 million PCs, and 2 million servers last year. If we can integrate all that information, it would enable us to know exactly how we are doing in Chicago on a given day, or whether the CIO of a big customer also happens to own any of our products at home."[5]

Given that HP is a company that primarily hires technical people, and technical people like to have their own machines and build their own systems, Mott's challenge from a cultural standpoint was huge. It was clear at the outset that a very large number of employees would need to be laid off, that a significant majority of the data centers would be eliminated, and that the number of supported systems would need to be cut by well over 50 percent. Peter Burrows of *Business Week* said, "Mott is testing the limits of the HP culture, taking away the rights of thousands of IT workers to purchase their own tech equipment."[6] Mott and Hurd were basically telling all these IT-savvy employees of HP to stop tinkering and fall in line, using corporate data, systems, and equipment standards.

The only way Mott was going to be able to achieve such significant change was with Hurd's total support. Too often, CIOs attempt to go it alone in implementing significant change because they know that when the situation gets tense, the CEO may not provide that backing. Going it alone is a huge mistake on the part of the CIO. The CEO needs to stand tall and totally back the effort, or the CIO will eventually fail. Mott knew this well and, thanks to his tight relationship with Hurd, had discussed this often with him and secured his total support.

One of the first steps that Mott took was to hire and place in key positions several talented IT professionals with whom he had prior relationships at Walmart and Dell.[7] Also, Hurd and Mott decided to take the whole project to HP's board of directors to enlist their commitment because it was obviously going to require significant investment to modernize and streamline HP from a systems standpoint. The board needed to understand that the target was to have five new data centers replace the existing eighty-five facilities and that new equipment costing tens of millions of dollars would be required to implement this plan.

Once the details of the plan were put together, the sheer magnitude of the cleanup job became apparent. Mott emerged with a plan for a three-year, $1 billion-plus overhaul of HP's IT environment. Along with the huge data center reduction, the eight hundred or so different databases would be discontinued and replaced by one corporation-wide data warehouse. Although this plan was both immense and costly, the payoff would be huge. Mott estimated that HP's annual expenditures on IT, $3.5 billion in 2005, would be cut by 50 percent in the future.[8]

When Mott arrived at HP, there were twelve hundred different IT projects being pursued; he quickly cut that down to five hundred. He also put stern project discipline in place to make sure that whatever projects IT did pursue were completed in a timely and efficient manner, and he consolidated the one hundred IT locations throughout the globe to twenty-five.[9] This was all totally new for HP.

In another critical step, Mott assigned, for each key corporate system, one person to be responsible for making and keeping that system minimal, effective, and standardized. That way Mott knew exactly whom to hold accountable to achieve the desired simplicity.

⬛ ⬛ ⬛

The kind of change that Mott effected at HP is not easy to accomplish. It takes clear vision, courage, and support to effectively simplify an overly complicated organization and also to prevent an organization from becoming overly complex in the first place. Here are some guidelines to keep in mind as you pursue that desired simplicity:

- *Put one leader in charge for each system or process.* For each system or process used to execute the business, you need to assign one strong individual as the leader, and charge that person to achieve the desired simplicity and effectiveness, just as Mott did at HP. The goal of the person responsible should be to standardize his or her assigned process across the whole company. Often individual business units and sales subsidiaries will make requests for unique features for their area, but agreeing to these requests needs to be a rarity, and well justified. Unfortunately, in most companies, the various functional areas that maintain these systems, such as finance, manufacturing, HR, or IT, often make the mistake of blindly implementing all special requests. It isn't long before things are fragmented and complicated. If one particular person is in charge of maintaining a particular system, he or she can keep this from happening.

- *Tell the organization.* The troops need to know that you have every intent of operating the organization in a simple manner and do not want to see processes and systems become complicated and bloated. They also need to know that for each system and process, one person is being put in charge and held accountable to achieve that desired simplicity.

- *Keep things simple and effective.* The person in charge of a particular system or process needs to constantly reevaluate his or her system or process and its role within the company, keeping an eye on how things can be kept simple and highly effective. This individual needs to fight off all the requests that come from various people in the organization wanting special bells and whistles added to the process. It's up to you as a leader to make sure that the person in charge of the process, and the entire organization, understand that the goal is simplicity and effectiveness.

- *Require 100 percent participation.* Both you and the individual you've put in charge of a particular process need to make it clear to everyone in the organization that the goal is to perform this process in one standardized way. The tendency within many organizations is for various divisions to go off and form their own fiefdoms and build their own systems and processes. It's up to you to continuously make it clear that such behavior is unacceptable and that every division within the company must use the same systems and processes. The goal is 100 percent participation. That is what Hurd and Mott made clear to the troops at HP.

Companies become incredibly complex over time, and it's usually reflected in their IT structure, with excess personnel, excess systems and databases, and so on, though it's likely that such complexity will also be present throughout the company. You need a very strong leader, such as Randy Mott at HP, to tackle these challenges and, most important, to keep systems and processes under control after they have been simplified and streamlined. The goal should always be to make the company, no matter how large it is, feel quite small. The ideal way to do that is with an absolute minimum number of standardized information systems that are used throughout the company. All the core processes that are used by all employees, be they HR programs, finance systems, or purchasing tools, should be performed one way and should be created with incredible simplicity by the particular functional organization and individual that are responsible.

# SINGLE-PERSON ACCOUNTABILITY

One lesson I've learned over the years is that if you put an employee who is intelligent, curious, and aggressive in a position where she is responsible for a key task and you make the goals very clear, you will be quite pleased with the results. She should be told to seek the input of others who she believes can provide her valuable information, but you need to make it very clear to her that she and she alone is accountable for the overall success for the effort. When you make things that clear, my experience is that there is an extremely high probability that this individual will perform very well.

What happens in many organizations, particularly as they hire more and more people, is that they become consensus oriented, and all kinds of people believe that they should participate in decisions and that their views should be reflected. Here is an example of how a good company can fall apart due to a lack of single-person accountability.

On December 1, 2006, it was announced that Alcatel, the French telecom equipment company, would merge with Lucent, a telecom equipment company in the United States. The CEO of Lucent at the time, Patricia Russo, would become the CEO of the newly merged company, and Serge Tchuruk, who had been the chairman and CEO of Alcatel for the prior twelve years, would be the nonexecutive chairman. The newly formed company would have combined revenue of $26 billion, and there was great expectation that it would emerge as a real global powerhouse.[10] The belief was that this newly created giant would be able to fight off the constant pricing pressure that was being exerted on all telecom equipment companies by their customers. From a financial perspective, the expectation was that large synergies would be achieved. At the time of the merger, the plan was to reduce headcount from a combined 80,000 to 67,500; that reduction plus other efficiencies would supposedly total $2.4 billion in annual cost savings.[11]

The merger was being positioned as a "marriage of equals."[12] However, not long after the announcement of the merger, it was becoming clear that the notion of a marriage of equals was quite problematic. That should have been a surprise to no one. In all organizations, it needs to be clear who is leading and making the decisions. That wasn't the case at Alcatel-Lucent.

Example after example demonstrated that Alcatel-Lucent was requiring both sides of the organization, Alcatel and Lucent, to agree with proposed changes. The company had even created "a vastly inflated executive committee with more than 20 members and a complex hierarchy that slowed down the whole decision-making process."[13] There was a lot of confusion regarding product lines, with supposedly discontinued lines still being sold by some teams.[14] And the problems extended much further, with "different parts of Alcatel-Lucent competing against each other in contract tenders, contributing to the price pressure that is crushing margins."[15] The company was in shambles.

As the business softened, the power struggle between Russo and Tchuruk began to become more obvious. It also became clear that Tchuruk, at age sixty-nine, was unwilling to give up power, and that there was a lack of accountability at the top because Tchuruk was keeping Russo from building her own team; in fact, "Tchuruk won the right in last minute negotiations to hold a veto over any operational appointments made by Miss Russo."[16]

All of this had very negative impact on the financial performance of the company; during 2007, three profit warnings were issued, and it was announced that the company would not hit its 5 percent sales growth target for 2007. In the last quarter of 2007, Alcatel-Lucent reported a loss of \$3.7 billion, which included a very large write-down as well as an operational loss.[17] Given these weak results, "the rationale for the merger and the credibility of the management are now in question."[18]

At the end of 2007, "customers, uncertain about possible changes in the merged company's product line-up, hesitated to place orders," and "many employees were distracted by worries their jobs would change or be eliminated," according to *Business Week*.[19] Obviously a lot of these problems were due to the incredibly slow pace of change at Alcatel-Lucent, no doubt because of the slow decision making throughout the company and the lack of clear accountability. Naturally, Alcatel-Lucent's competitors, Ericsson and Huawei, viewed the slow movement of Alcatel-Lucent as a huge opportunity and jumped all over it, gaining significant market share in the wireless network business.

As 2007 came to a close, comments from the press in regard to Alcatel-Lucent's problems in decision making became more specific: "Difficult strategic choices will have to be made that may offend either party—such as site closures or consolidation of research and development centers—and that will spark political controversy on one side of the Atlantic or the other."[20] By early 2008, Alcatel-Lucent's market value had plunged more than \$20 billion from the time of the merger and was below the book value of the company.

▨ ▨ ▨

Alcatel-Lucent provides a vivid example of what happens when decision-making authority is not clear. Single-person accountability is crucial to make an organization run well. It's very surprising that the seasoned executives from these two companies allowed this kind of behavior to go on. History suggests, however, that positioning an acquisition as a merger of equals rarely works because it confuses who is actually accountable.

Unfortunately Alcatel-Lucent is just one example of many. I've seen these sorts of problems happen over and over again, leading me to believe strongly in the following key lessons:

- *Make one person responsible.* As I discussed in the HP case, better results occur when one person knows that the buck stops with him and that success or failure will be connected directly to him. It also speeds things up and causes the person responsible to be more thorough because his reputation is on the line. The wasted time and effort in our Alcatel-Lucent example as Tchuruk and Russo both struggled not to lose control certainly make the point.

- *Don't allow consensus decision making.* Requiring consensus causes leaders to begin believing that their most important task is asking a whole bunch of other people what should be done. A plan is then formulated and executed mostly because everyone agrees on it. The seductive part of this approach is that it lets leaders off the hook; they are not really responsible for the end result. If things go wrong in one particular area, the leader can appropriately blame the group, saying "They gave bad information and advice." Even worse, the individuals who are asked to be involved in a consensus decision often put that effort at a low to medium priority and don't do a quality job of providing input, because they are not really accountable. Further, leaders believe that they don't have to do their own research because other people will do it for them. Don't let this happen in your organization. It is a guaranteed recipe for mediocrity. Be sure that you make one person clearly responsible for each project and outcome.

- *Beware of meddling bosses.* I often see situations where an individual is given a set of responsibilities but that individual's boss constantly provides advice in such a way that it is interpreted as an order. The individual quickly concludes that the way to make the boss happy is to simply listen, provide a little pushback when there is lack of agreement, but then do what the boss wants. Unfortunately, this puts the individual in an extremely vulnerable situation. Although the boss may be providing advice, the project is ultimately the employee's responsibility, and by not taking a more active role in the project, the employee is setting himself up for failure. It is shocking how many organizations create situations where a manager gets so involved in projects assigned to his team that the people to whom the projects are actually delegated feel such immense pressure to please the boss that they lose sight of what they are trying to accomplish.

When you delegate a responsibility to a member of your team, make sure that person has the freedom to run with his own ideas. Sure you can check in on the project to be certain it's focused, but don't force the project to be done a specific way. You've chosen this person to handle the project because he is a high performer and you trust him to get the right results. So let him!

- *Remain strong willed, thorough, and objective.* When a leader receives input on a proposal that she is responsible for, she must realize that those providing the input may be biased and have a vested interest in a particular outcome. Leaders need to be strong willed enough to constantly push and probe to understand the input they are being provided to make sure it's not just a defensive input to protect the existing practices from change. They must also be objective enough not only to reject bad input but to acknowledge and accept good input without letting their own biases get in the way. In the Alcatel-Lucent example, Russo was prevented from being a thorough, objective leader, the most striking examples being her inability to build her own team and Tchuruk's having veto power over operational appointments.

Courageous leaders know that single-person accountability is a must. Use these guidelines to make sure you know where responsibility lies within your organization at all times. It's the only way to achieve reliable results.

# MINIMUM LAYERS AND MAXIMUM SPANS

With time, organizations tend to add layers and decrease the span of control of managers. This typically happens because they want to promote people, and creating new bosses and layers is a natural way to do that: you're not really promoting them, but the organization chart shows you are. Because the new bosses often lack management experience, you limit the number of people reporting to them. This section deals with just how bad the problem of excess layers can get, the difficulties that excess layers cause, and a description of an ideal structure from a spans-and-layers point of view.

### Bloated Organizations

During the years 2000 through 2004, Andrea Jung did a terrific job as the leader of Avon. The company's annual revenue increased from $5.3 to $7.7 billion, and profits increased by a factor of three.[21] This 120-year-old company was really on a roll. Its stock price moved from $16 per share in January 2000 to $43 per share at the end of 2004.

Starting in 2005, Avon began to have serious problems. During its period of success, it had hired a lot of people, and its organization became quite complex. By early 2006, Avon had an astounding fifteen organizational layers. That has to be some kind of world record! Also, its business was really suffering. Avon's North American revenue decreased for six consecutive quarters. Its stock fell accordingly, hitting $25 per share in October 2005.

Besides the complexity in the company's management structure, the sheer number of items Avon was offering to its customers exploded. It was adding roughly a thousand products annually to what was already a huge list. For example, its product list in Mexico had grown to thirteen thousand items. In 2005, 82 percent of Avon's sales of beauty products were discounted in price to assist in making sales. The need for discounting typically signals weak, nondistinctive products. Given all the excess staffing and the complicated set of layers, Avon's overhead reached $2.5 billion.[22]

This sort of bloating is not rare. In the early 1990s, the perennially successful Procter & Gamble faced a major concern because its growing sales and administrative costs were becoming too large a percentage of its revenue. I was a senior vice president at that juncture, and was chosen to head up a team to tackle this spans-and-layers problem. What we found was that P&G had gotten more complicated than it should have, with up to ten layers between the CEO and the entry-level personnel in P&G's various line and staff divisions. Equally important, the spans of control had grown excessively narrow. By "span" here, I'm talking about the number of people who report to a manager. At the lower levels, there were many managers who had only one or two people reporting to them.

Clearly one of the reasons why this was occurring was the pressure to promote people who had been with the company a fair number of years. As I mentioned earlier, the tendency in these cases is to create an extra layer of management and have only a few people report to the newly promoted, quite inexperienced managers.

### The Resulting Problems

Excess layers and narrow spans can cause some major issues in an organization. Here are the most serious ones:

- *Slow decision making.* In an organization with excessive layers of management, it just takes more work and more time to plow through those layers to get to the approval level you need. It takes time to set up meetings, send all those e-mails, and wait for responses. And oftentimes the people whose responses you are awaiting don't have the same sense of urgency that you do. Streamlining your organization's management levels cuts down on decision-making time so that people can accomplish tasks more quickly and efficiently.
- *Fogged-up communications.* Involving more people in resolving an issue means increasing your chances of getting off track and wasting a lot of time. That's what excess layers do. Everyone involved feels

compelled to come up with his or her own unique input; and with every additional person involved, the chances of there being misunderstandings increase.

- *Dangerous meddling*. Managers with narrow spans of control simply have too much time on their hands, so they end up sticking their noses into their direct reports' business and micromanaging. Accountability can become quite vague when a manager spends a significant amount of time involved in the efforts of his or her direct reports.

### The Ideal

One of the key principles that should underpin the span-and-layers structure of any organization is that as managers gain more experience, they should be able to handle an increasing number of direct reports. As noted in Table 4.1, a very reasonable structure is to assume that your first-level manager will have a minimum of four direct reports. That's not a big load, but it's large enough to keep the manager from meddling too much in his or her direct reports' business.

As you then go up the chain of levels, you can slightly increase that minimum number of direct reports for each level. It's always debated as to what is the best number of direct reports for a highly experienced

**Table 4.1** Organizational Layers

| Level | Span of Control | Number of People at the Level |
|---|---|---|
| 1 (CEO) | 8 | 1 |
| 2 | 8 | 8 |
| 3 | 8 | 64 |
| 4 | 7 | 512 |
| 5 | 6 | 3, 584 |
| 6 | 4 | 21,504 |
| 7 (entry level) | | 86,016 |
| **Total** | | **111,668** |

manager at an executive level. Certainly eight direct reports should be quite manageable; in my opinion, the target should be between eight and ten.

The best way to understand the table is to start at the top, at the CEO level. We have one person at that level, and he or she has eight direct reports. Those eight folks at level 2 each have eight direct reports, so that means there are sixty-four people at level 3. You get the idea.

One thing that is important to note about your "target" spans-and-layers structure is that it dictates the number of people you can handle within your organization. For example, in Table 4.1, we are quite conservative with respect to the number of direct reports per manager when the manager is younger, and then we increase that number to eight for the higher levels. With this structure, you see that we can accommodate a total of 111,688 personnel. This is the chart that convinced us at P&G that we were clearly being too sloppy with our spans and layers. For example, the total P&G organization was about a hundred thousand people, and the various divisions and functions were operating with nine to ten layers. The first list following shows the typical advertising organization in a P&G international subsidiary. In the second list, you see the IT organization, which utilized ten layers. Clearly, both had too many layers.

*Procter & Gamble—Europe Division, Germany Subsidiary, Advertising Organization*

1. CEO
2. Executive VP of international
3. Group VP of Europe
4. Regional VP of Western Europe
5. VP of Germany
6. Advertising manager
7. Associate advertising manager
8. Brand manager
9. Assistant brand managers and brand assistants

In the new design, layers 3 and 7 were eliminated.

*P&G, Corporate Information Technology*

1. CEO
2. Senior VP
3. VP of information technology
4. Department heads
5. Function managers
6. Section heads
7. Group managers
8. Unit managers
9. Project leader
10. Analysts

In the new design, layers 5, 8, and 9 were eliminated.

## How Did Avon and P&G Fix Things?

In the case of Avon, CEO Jung began to tackle the problem with gusto in early 2006. She decreased the number of management layers from fifteen down to seven or eight.[23] This was part of a major restructuring that took out $500 million of cost, and she used a fair amount of the savings to increase Avon's ad spending.[24] Inadequate advertising was viewed as one of the core issues in Avon's business softness, besides all the complexity it was putting up with internally. Jung also eliminated 25 percent of the company's products and increased the Avon sales reps' typical compensation in key markets.[25]

All these smart moves by Avon generated a 6 percent sales growth in 2006 and put its stock back on a growth track: its stock moved from $28 in early 2006 to the $40 range by late 2007.

P&G tackled its complexity issue through a number of steps focused on reducing complexity and bureaucracy. One of the key thrusts was to adopt spans-and-layers targets that were very similar to what you see in Table 4.1. As noted following the earlier lists, two of the nine layers of the typical P&G international subsidiary were eliminated, and corporate IT went from ten to seven layers. P&G used the pattern in Table 4.1 as a benchmark to significantly streamline the organization.

## The Technical Ladder

One thing that a lot of companies do to avoid the pressure to add extra layers is to create a separate ladder for the technical community, one with titles and pay raises that are on par with the managerial ladder. This is so that people who are very good at what they do but shouldn't become managers have a way to progress in the company. Separate ladders avoid the dual problems of poor management by people not cut out for the job and of sending the harmful message that technical work is not as valued as managerial work.

In creating a technical or dual ladder, it is important to make sure that the pay structures are roughly equal for both ladders. If you don't, it won't be long before the technical community gets up in arms because they are being shortchanged. This means that you need to set fairly high standards when you decide to promote someone to the next level on the technical ladder, just as you would on a managerial ladder. The individual needs to be a significant contributor to the success of the organization.

The big advantage of a technical ladder is that it creates a culture where there are multiple ways to succeed. Becoming a manager isn't the ultimate goal. There are a lot of people who simply shouldn't take a managerial career route, but they believe they are forced to do so because that is the only way to progress in the company.

▨▨▨

The issue of spans and layers is very important. It dictates the speed and efficiency with which you can deal with change and tackle your markets. There is nothing more frustrating than wading through levels of managers and bureaucracy in order to get approval to do something you know is right for your organization. Take the spans-and-layers issue very seriously when striving for simplicity in your organization.

# 5

## PRINCIPLE IV

# Institutionalize Tight-Fisted Cost Control

In general, most employees and managers believe that they need more people in order to get their work done. They also need more equipment, more systems, more of everything. Because of this inherent human tendency to bulk up, a leader needs to be tough, objective, and very visible regarding cost. He needs to be constantly working to make his organization very lean and cost conscious. It requires guts, but it's essential. As a leader, you must take a very clear and continual stand on the need for tight-fisted cost management.

In recent years, I worked with a company that was considering outsourcing as a means of cutting costs. Outsourcing has become an obvious tool for gaining efficiency in those parts of an operation that aren't strategic. I was working with a consumer electronics business, specifically the VP of manufacturing. The consumer electronics industry had changed significantly in the previous five years. Incredibly capable and efficient outsourcing alternatives popped up throughout Asia to produce products not only more efficiently but also in a more flexible and timely manner.

The VP of manufacturing with whom I was working had spent his entire career in the manufacturing area and took tremendous pride in his twenty years of experience and his breadth of knowledge with regard to manufacturing practices in the consumer electronics industry. The CEO of the company was concerned that most of the company's competitors were using Asian vendors to make their products and asked me to work with this VP to figure out if the company was missing an opportunity to cut costs.

In my first meeting with the VP, he was quite cordial and very open in explaining the nature of his responsibilities and giving me an in-depth look into his expertise and the depth of manufacturing talent that resided within the company. He had charts galore focused on the defect rates and the costs of outsourcing versus manufacturing internally. His argument was that the expertise in his organization was so deep that it had both a cost and quality advantage over outsourcers. During that first meeting, I listened intently and collected all the sheets of data for further review.

A month later, I was back at the company and had a lot of questions about the data and the nature of the outsource vendors that had been used in the benchmarking. The VP was quite emotional and very aggressive when I tried to thoroughly review the cost data he had given me and when I attempted to discuss possible advantages of outsourcing. He refused to consider the possibility of outsourcing and wouldn't engage in conversation regarding the cost benefits all his major competitors were gaining from using outside vendors.

Finally, I simply suggested that it would be smart to take one of the company's products and to produce a portion of it with one of these vendors to see what the actual costs and quality were. I clearly hit a nerve, and the VP became extremely defensive and highly critical of my line of questioning. I stuck to my position and continued to ask why he was unwilling to try such an experiment. He completely dismissed my suggestions. What I was seeing here was a lack of leadership on cost. Later in the day, I met with the CEO to review the conversation and discuss my frustration, and I suggested that he set forth an ultimatum: either some experimentation be done, or a change of personnel would need to be considered. The CEO said he thought that was a great idea.

A month later, I was back visiting the company, and I found out that the CEO never had that conversation. What a shame. The CEO could have simply decided to do some testing, and I again pushed that option, but it was obvious that he wasn't going to take a stand. Strong leadership was a must, and this CEO just wasn't up to the challenge. I did notice that one year later, when that company had gotten itself into serious profit problems, one of the high-profile decisions it made was to close down all its consumer electronics manufacturing and move it to an outsource vendor in Asia. Some of those profit problems could have been avoided altogether if the CEO had just exercised leadership on cost before the situation became so bad.

Confronting the status quo and making tight-fisted cost control a key priority are hard; they require courageous leadership and backbone. People always want more: more people, higher salaries, more systems, more equipment, and on and on. In the following sections, I will discuss three important initiatives for you to use in institutionalizing tight-fisted cost control.

## TAKE A TOUGH, VISIBLE STAND ON COST

Keeping costs down is a continual battle. Budgets can be very emotional topics in organizations; when talk of freezing or squeezing a budget, terminating a languishing project, or outsourcing a specific activity surfaces, you are guaranteed to experience some very strong and violent reactions. People take budgets personally. A leader can't manage cost by just trying to squeeze here or there. She needs to very visibly tell the organization, over and over, that cost control is a key priority and that all employees and managers will be held responsible to help institutionalize tight-fisted cost management.

Following are two examples of leaders trying to gain control over spending. In the first situation, the leader, the CEO of Nestlé, manages to make cost a priority and achieves major success. In the second situation, the CIO of a major auto-parts manufacturer fails to take a strong stand on cost, and all plans for cost cutting fail. There are lessons to be learned from both.

Peter Brabeck, the CEO of Nestlé, is a great example of a strong leader striving for tight-fisted cost control. In the year 2000, Brabeck faced some real challenges. Although the company's financial results were decent, the organization had gotten absolutely huge, and the resulting costs created by excess headcount, manufacturing facilities, and individual products were no longer acceptable. Nestlé had 230,000 employees operating in seventy countries, and marketed over eight thousand individual products. It also had just under five hundred manufacturing facilities, twice that of Unilever, the global consumer products giant.[1]

Brabeck announced to the entire company that his number one goal was to tackle Nestlé's cost problem and achieve industry-leading operational efficiency.[2] Naming cost management and operational efficiency as the number one goal sent a clear message to every member of Nestlé. The way the company operated was going to have to change.

Brabeck had clear authority to drive change. However, it was important for him to make sure his board of directors knew what he was doing and totally agreed to support his plans. The board needed to understand that Brabeck's efforts would result in layoffs and possible plant closings that would generate negative publicity for the company. They were enthusiastic about attacking the increasingly problematic key cost issues, and Brabeck very publicly launched his tight-fisted cost control efforts.

In his attempts to cut costs and simplify structures, Brabeck discovered a wide variety of problems within Nestlé. The company's structure had become "decentralized," and country managers had been given too much "leeway on everything from purchasing to capital investments."[3] Naturally, some of those investments were in local systems and processes, complicating the ability of the company to operate uniformly and efficiently across all its far-reaching groups. For example, there were a large variety of local approaches to procurement. Problems were so bad that "different factories were using different names for the identical grade of sugar, making it almost impossible for bosses at headquarters to track cost."[4]

Also, Nestlé's American factories were all purchasing raw materials independently, and "as a result, the company sometimes paid more than 20 different prices for vanilla purchased from the same supplier" according to the *Economist*.[5] Because each factory identified vanilla with a different code, bosses at the Glendale, California, headquarters could not spot this very obvious problem.

By 2003, Brabeck was well into his efforts to simplify things. As he pursued his efficiency goal, he tackled much of this duplication by selecting certain functional areas, such as purchasing, and forcing the various countries to move to a unified set of systems and processes. He also forced individual countries into regional units in order to gain efficiencies. For example, New Zealand, Australia, and the Pacific Islands were consolidated into one regional unit that moved to single accounting, administration, sales, and payroll systems. These moves may not have been popular with everyone, but such pushback is natural. When organizations fragment, those fragments get used to a certain amount of independence and will fight off any efforts to take that independence away.

Brabeck didn't just focus on the small countries and markets; he also tackled the inefficiencies within large countries. In the United States, he demanded standardized approaches. For example, Nestlé USA had twenty-one thousand employees, $12 billion in sales, and forty-two factories across the country. Those factories had operated quite independently, and Brabeck had to put common IT systems and standardized processes into place across all the Nestlé USA operations.

Brabeck launched a significant effort to clean up Nestlé's information systems mess. The program was called Global Business Excellence.[6] This was an implementation of SAP software throughout the company, and its goal was to achieve one information technology platform across the entire company, standardizing packaging codes and providing more accurate data on virtually all aspects of the company. This was a massive effort on the part of Nestlé and one of the main components of Brabeck's operational efficiency thrust.

The kind of cost and operational complexity that had emerged within Nestlé is more the norm than an exception. Organizations tend to fragment, the numerous resulting groups go off in their own directions, and costs increase significantly. You need strong leaders like Peter Brabeck to tackle such tendencies and institutionalize tight-fisted cost control.

■ ■ ■

The second example involves an auto-parts manufacturer with $10 billion in annual revenue. It's an engineering-based organization that had seven independent operating divisions, all of which had become very accustomed to their independence. Profits were in trouble primarily because costs were out of control. The management of the company was under tremendous pressure because the stock price had been losing about 10 percent of its value each year for the past three years. Its biggest problem was that the company spent 6.4 percent of its revenue on information technology when the benchmark for IT spending in the industry was 3.0 percent.

The CEO of the organization approved a plan developed by the CIO to implement one set of financial, HR, and manufacturing information systems across the organization. The CIO had proposed a two-year project plan that would cut IT costs by at least 50 percent. The CEO strongly endorsed the effort publicly, and the CIO went to work on the implementation.

Given that the seven operating divisions were very independent and full of engineering-oriented people, each had its own information systems and a never-ending list of modifications to any corporate systems to meet its special needs. The CIO's attempt to implement one set of systems in finance, HR, and manufacturing was met with tremendous pushback. Those operating divisions thought that the spirit of the company was to allow each of its operating divisions to run its own business and be responsible for its own destiny and that this plan violated that spirit. Each department had elegant explanations as to why its particular costs were a bit high, and they all tried to push the problems off onto the other divisions, agreeing that those divisions were clearly operating with excessive costs.

Several of these operating divisions confronted the CEO and CIO and complained that they were being mistreated. One by one, these operating divisions got the CEO to agree to make exceptions here and there. As the various divisions realized that the CEO was willing to back off and that they could keep their independence, the CIO was inundated with requests for special treatment by the operating divisions so that their world be minimally impacted.

Not surprisingly, given the CEO's behavior, none of the cost efforts within the company made much progress, and its financial performance continued to falter. It wasn't long before the board of directors had no choice but to relieve the CEO of his duties and hire a new leader.

▨▨▨

So how can you avoid the fate of the CEO of the auto-parts manufacturer and achieve the kind of success that Brabeck did at Nestlé? Here are some key guidelines that you need to follow to take a stand on complexity and achieve tight-fisted cost control.

- *Take a tough, visible stand on cost.* The troops need to know you are making cost management a high priority. You need to send this message over and over. Use all the communication tools available to you to constantly reinforce the message.
- *Match your actions to your words.* Don't allow exceptions that will be talked about in the halls that clearly show you are willing to back off the cost objective, as the CEO at the auto-parts manufacturer did. Employees will be watching closely to learn how they can best protect their assets and ideally acquire more.
- *Take budgeting seriously.* Know your budget well. As the leader, you need to be very thorough in scrutinizing each element of your budget. The planning and budgeting process must also be interactive so that the troops clearly understand your thinking. They must understand why you are making certain financial decisions and what pressures you are facing, which will enable them to trust that you are being an objective and effective leader.

- *Be prepared for faultfinding.* One of the toughest things to do in an organization is to constrain or tighten resources. It brings out some of the worst emotions in people that you can imagine. You and managers who report to you will need to be prepared for criticism and faultfinding. At times your determination will be perceived as rudeness and stubbornness, but you can't let this affect your decision. You must constantly remind folks why you are doing this in the first place. You and your team will need to be very gutsy leaders, just as Brabeck was at Nestlé.

As a leader, you need to be very clear and very visible with plans and rationale for achieving tight-fisted budgets. You also need to continually reinforce the message that cost is very important. That's how you institutionalize aggressive cost management.

## FIX OR KILL OBVIOUS COST BLUNDERS

Organizations often try to do too much. This can get them in trouble. Once an idea is born and staffed, it is hard to stop. The people involved will fight passionately to keep the effort going, because they believe in the project but also, more important, because they fear for their job if the project is stopped. Success often leads to sloppiness in cost and focus and can result in the pursuit of unnecessary projects. This leads to excessive cost, complexity, and distractions that can sap the productivity of an organization. Ideally, companies can prevent this from happening, but when it does happen, fixing or killing these cost blunders requires a leader to be strong.

Volkswagen made numerous mistakes in this area and is a good example of how a company can get into deep financial trouble because of significant cost blunders it refuses to fix.

Ferdinand Piëch was the CEO of Volkswagen from 1993 to 2002. Piëch reinvigorated VW in the mid-1990s by launching the new VW Beetle and introducing a new design and manufacturing efficiency approach that enabled VW to make more models that had the same parts.[7] Unfortunately, his last few years as CEO did not go nearly as well. By the time Piëch retired in April 2002, Volkswagen was losing market share to Japanese and European manufacturers, profits were declining, and the company had too many different brands and models, some of which were quite expensive and had not performed well in the marketplace at all. In the year prior to Piëch's retirement, sales fell 2 percent and operating profits fell 12 percent. VW had also warned the financial markets that the results in 2002 would be worse. Clearly Piëch had lost the focus on cost and profit growth and was fascinated with launching new models.[8]

One of the most significant mistakes Piëch made was the $1 billion effort in the late 1990s to get into the luxury car business.[9] He tried to make that vision a reality by developing a top-of-the-line VW called the Phaeton, priced at $75,000, that would compete with BMW and Mercedes, while also pursuing the ultra luxury–sports car segment by buying Bentley, Bugatti, and Lamborghini. He even approved construction of a $200 million glass-walled factory in Dresden to build this new luxury model. The factory could build up to 150 Phaetons per day and had the annual capacity of over forty thousand.[10] But in its first fifteen months, only fifty one hundred Phaetons were sold; the press reported that Volkswagen was said to be losing $69 million a year on Phaeton.[11]

Piëch also launched work to develop a new $1.3 million Bugatti model that would achieve speeds of almost 250 miles per hour, which is faster than Formula One cars.[12] The incremental revenue in the luxury segment is very small because you don't sell many cars, yet Volkswagen was spending billions to break into this market. What was a $100 billion car company doing spending big money and management time on projects that would generate negligible revenue? The lack of focus here on basic cost and profit management was really striking.

Volkswagen should have been using its engineering staff to upgrade popular models such as the Golf and Passat and to launch hot new products in the SUV and multipurpose category. Very simply, VW needed to make more cars that buyers want to buy. As noted in

*Fortune,* "Piëch's approach created too many hatchbacks, knotchbacks, and longbacks, and too few SUVs, minivans, roadsters, and other profitable lifestyle niches that Volkswagen missed."[13] Piëch also pushed hard for an eight-cylinder Passat when the marketplace said that Passat buyers were simply not interested in a high-powered vehicle, especially one carrying the VW name. Some simple consumer research should have been able to quantitatively verify that—before VW spent big money to pursue such a project. The obvious cost blunders by VW in the later 1990s were actually quite staggering.

Volkswagen had other big cost issues. For example, the state of Lower Saxony, which owned 18 percent of Volkswagen shares, was more concerned with preserving jobs at Volkswagen facilities in its area than it was with Volkswagen profits. Lower Saxony pressured Volkswagen into putting manufacturing facilities in some of the most expensive geographies in the world. This was a major cost blunder.

Another major revenue and profit issue was that Volkswagen treated the U.S. market as second priority. As *Fortune* said, "it used the country [the United States] as a dumping ground for excess production and made little effort to understand American driving habits. A classic example: cup holders, which for years VW ignored."[14] And although an updated version of the VW Golf was introduced in Europe in October 2003, it wasn't launched in the United States until almost three years later.

There was a severe lack of discipline at VW regarding its project portfolio and an unwillingness even to acknowledge cost blunders, let alone fix them, but the company paid the price. Its profits declined by 32 percent in 2003. This had big negative implications for its stock, which was trading at $104 per share in the late 1990s but then bounced around $30 to $60 for the next five years.[15]

▨ ▨ ▨

It's easy for us to see now what VW should have done to avoid these major cost problems. But clearly it wasn't obvious to VW at the time. Piëch turned a blind eye to some major cost blunders, but you don't have to do the same. Here are some things a gutsy leader needs to do to avoid these kinds of problems and kill them immediately when they do arise:

- *Be reluctant to launch new efforts.* Before allowing a project to be born, you as a leader must demand extensive data and very clear strategic arguments. This isn't to say that you should never launch new efforts, but you must be hypercritical and exacting when examining the business case for a new project. Is the project feasible? What's the ROI? Be sure that every project has strong potential cost savings, profit potential, or both. What are the risks? What is the worst-case scenario? If you have issues after all this probing, kill the project before it starts. Obviously VW failed miserably on this point.

- *Have a regularly scheduled, objective process for killing projects.* You need to meet regularly with project leaders to review projects. The timing should depend on the size and stage of development of each particular project. If you are at an urgent stage where big funding is needed or test results are coming in, then perhaps review weekly. At less critical stages, you may meet for review less often. Figure out how frequently it makes sense to meet to review a project, set a schedule for review, and stick to it. If the project isn't on course and meeting expectations, kill it. Remember, people will come up with ingenious ways to defend their projects. They often become emotionally involved with their work and may truly believe that what they are doing has promise. It is your job to be objective and stubborn, to regularly question current efforts, and to kill what isn't working.

- *Decrease your enrollment levels when you eliminate a project.* Often when a project is terminated, the people who were involved will be placed on other projects or allowed to start something new. When this happens, you miss a big opportunity for trimming down your organization. You continue to carry bloated cost and complexity. When you kill a project, the people should either be placed in a current vacancy, be moved to replace a poor performer who is being terminated, or let go. This sort of discipline requires a lot of courage on your part, but it's the only way to keep your costs down and keep your organization tightly focused on the things that are going to make a big difference.

A gutsy leader must constantly look at her operation in an objective manner to avoid or immediately fix or kill any obvious cost blunders she sees. You need to be ruthless with yourself and others when it comes to deciding which projects merit moving forward and which current projects must die. Failure to be so can result in the kind of catastrophe that Volkswagen experienced, or worse.

## BE GLOBAL

With any organization, no matter what the size, you are constantly faced with the question of where tasks should be done. Hire an outsource vendor? Staff up and do it internally? In what country? Obviously, the key factors that come into play are cost, existing talent within the organization, the availability of vendors who could perform the task, and the strategic nature of the particular task. The key point to remember is to think globally as you make these evaluations. Your competition is! With today's telecommunications capabilities; low-cost, high-quality manufacturing and product development capabilities around the world; and countries willing to provide attractive tax packages, it is imperative to be global, even if you are a small company.

IBM is truly a global organization. But before its global integration, each of the IBM subsidiaries in over 150 countries operated as a stand-alone entity. These subsidiaries staffed whatever skills were needed to meet the needs of customers in that geographic area. This was quite expensive because resources were often duplicated or underutilized in a particular country.[16]

Between 2005 and 2007, IBM moved to what it calls its globally integrated enterprise model. Using this model, IBM executes particular tasks in a particular country by drawing on talent that could be located anywhere within the IBM Corporation or, if the activity is not strategic, could be done by any of its qualified outsource vendors throughout the world. The general rule is to get the right talent at the right price to do the task, not just to use the staff and resources within a country because it seems easier.[17]

Moving to this new model has had huge organizational implications for IBM. For example, IBM has hired an estimated ninety thousand people and placed them in low-cost global service delivery centers (GSDCs) in such countries as Brazil, China, and India. The people in these GSDCs perform a wide variety of activities—such as computer programming, data center operations, help desk customer response, accounting, and benefits management services—that IBM requires to meet the needs of its customers around the world.[18] Naturally, inexpensive labor was the key driver in setting up this model, as wages in a country such as India can be 70 to 80 percent lower than in the United States. IBM has found that in these low-cost countries, it can hire fully qualified people to do a broad variety of tasks.[19] This is not just about cheap manufacturing.

The globally integrated enterprise model has caused massive shifts in the geographical distribution of IBM's talent. IBM cut fifteen thousand jobs across the United States, Europe, and Japan in order to set up resources in low-cost countries.[20] But the savings for IBM have been huge. In the manufacturing supply chain alone, IBM saved $5 billion of annual costs by moving to a global model.[21] It used to be that IBM factories produced a limited number of products for a particular country. Today, IBM manufacturing centers produce a wide variety of products for a wide variety of countries. This enables the company to operate with far fewer plants that run at a much higher capacity.

This same principle of consolidating operations and moving them to low-cost countries was applied to the services area when setting up the GDSCs. The main factors considered in choosing the locations were cost, available talent, educational pipelines, languages spoken, proximity to markets, and political stability; the end result was that IBM's finance and administrative back-office centers moved to Bangalore, Buenos Aires, Krakow, Shanghai, and Tulsa.[22]

IBM's new global form presented a challenging task. When your employees, along with their talents, skills, and capabilities, are distributed all over the globe, how do you keep it all straight? How can you be sure that you are assigning the best resources at the lowest cost to a particular task? To assist in doing that, IBM created new databases that contain records of each employee, his or her capabilities, and his or her up-to-the-minute availability. These databases are kept up-to-date by employees and their managers and contain all the facts necessary to understand what any given individual can contribute to a specific project. This isn't just about skills; the databases also factor in cost and availability. When a task emerges within IBM, a manager can go to a database and conduct a variety of searches to find the person best suited to the task at hand. IBM claims that just one of these databases, the Professional Marketplace, has enabled the company to shorten the average time it takes to assemble a team to work on a project by 20 percent.[23] These databases are also used to project what kind of talent needs to be recruited, by noting what talent is in supply and what the recent demands have been. When shortages are spotted, locations are selected for the recruiting task based on the availability and cost of talent in that area.

The staffing in the GSDCs significantly increased as IBM got used to this new global model. IBM Brazil saw its employment level go from four thousand people to thirteen thousand in the five years between 2002 and 2007. Most of these people work in the global service delivery center near São Paulo. This group has a wide variety of skills, and their language capabilities include English, French, Portuguese, and Spanish. In this Brazilian GSDC, wages are about 50 percent of what IBM would have to pay in the United States.[24]

IBM has truly become a globally integrated enterprise. When decisions need to be made regarding whether or not to outsource a task, IBM talent throughout the world is considered. The decision is then driven purely by skill level and cost.[25]

Becoming global isn't simply something that is appropriate only for companies like IBM with hundreds of thousands of employees. Even small companies should be thinking this way. Although small companies won't have people spread all around the globe, they can outsource nonstrategic tasks and should look globally to find the vendor that will provide the best work at the lowest cost.

IBM converted from fragmented to globally integrated with near seamlessness, but this isn't always easy to do. There are some basic rules you should follow when you start thinking globally. Again, it doesn't matter what size your organization is; you can be as big as IBM or just starting up. Either way, the same rules apply:

- *Consider outsourcing nonstrategic activities.* Nonstrategic. activities are those tasks that aren't going to give you a competitive advantage, things like administering a benefits program, or manufacturing products that don't require highly specialized expertise. There are vendors throughout the world that would gladly take on these tasks and have expertise in these areas. There is no doubt that outsource vendors need to be managed carefully with well-thought-out performance criteria, but they can also provide services at a low cost and at a high quality level, making it very cost-effective for most companies.
- *Choose the right location for strategic activities.* Strategic activities affect the nature of your products and services. The marketing and positioning of your products are strategic because they affect the way a product is received in the marketplace. Where to locate strategic activities is an important decision. The world has gotten small. Up-to-date communications capabilities allow you to tap into global expertise and lower costs. A start-up in Silicon Valley might decide to put an office in India where its key software developers can create the company's core applications. This start-up saves a lot of money while also tapping into the deep global expertise in software development that resides in India. Examine the needs of your business to decide if putting some of your strategic activities in

an international office would make sense. This is exactly what IBM did in setting itself up as a globally integrated enterprise.

- *Be strong*. Whether you're outsourcing your nonstrategic activities or setting up a global office to handle some strategic ones, chances are that your organization will aggressively fight these decisions. These decisions may save money, but they may also cost jobs. Employees will argue that the company has unique expertise to do the tasks or that the tasks require intimate knowledge that only they have. As a leader, you need to be aware that this pressure will always be there, and you need to be tough.

When you begin talking about outsourcing or relocating internal efforts to low-cost countries, you should expect people to become upset and push back. But if you are truly going to institute a tight-fisted cost mentality in your organization and drive your profitability ahead of your competition in today's world, you need to approach business in a truly global manner, no matter what the size of your company. Your competition will be, and you'll suffer big-time if you don't think globally as well.

# 6

## PRINCIPLE V

# Insist on Functional Excellence

As leaders get promoted and gain more responsibility in an organization, they simply can't immediately acquire all the in-depth knowledge required to fully understand every area that falls within their authority. The higher an individual moves in the organization, the truer this becomes. In order to ensure functional excellence, leaders need to have very talented, courageous, and highly principled individuals working for them. These people need to have in-depth knowledge of their field and must be willing to challenge the boss when they don't agree. This is particularly true in skill-dependent functional areas like manufacturing, IT, finance, and HR. When leaders lack knowledge and also lack someone who can be a reliable source of knowledge, things get messy. Huge amounts of complexity are caused all the time by sloppy functional leaders and sloppy practices. It is often the major source of operational chaos in an organization.

I once was in a meeting where the CEO asked a VP of a particular operating division how many manufacturing people there were in his division. The corporate finance guy in attendance immediately pulled up on his PC the manufacturing headcount data in the corporate finance database and said 845. The director of HR for the division responded quickly saying that the corporate finance director was wrong and that the data she had in front of her from HR's more accurate database indicated that the number was 819. She also said that the corporate finance database was always out-of-date regarding headcount and should not be trusted, thus incensing the corporate finance person. The divisional director of manufacturing then jumped in and claimed that each division's manufacturing unit had its own process for tracking its employee base and that the proper way to answer the question was to get the number from that division's manufacturing database. He indicated that his factsheet printed from that database indicated that the number was 814. By this time, steam was coming out of the CEO's ears. What he was experiencing is a typical example of just how complex, fragmented, and sloppy a company can become. Unfortunately, I had the nasty job of telling the CEO after the meeting that it was his fault!

If you think about this example, the problems are obvious. There was clearly no single "headcount database" and no single person or even department in charge of that function. In the case of headcount, HR should be held accountable. HR is guilty here for allowing the fragmentation of a set of core corporate data—namely, a corporate personnel database. Clearly, tough HR leadership was lacking. Even though HR is usually in charge of payroll systems, manufacturing went and developed its own, but unfortunately, manufacturing was fragmented so badly that there were even multiple payroll systems across the various divisions. Losing control of payroll practices and other core databases, processes, and systems not only is an operational and cost disaster but can lead to legal issues. Things weren't any better in finance or IT; the operating divisions were off doing their own thing. The place was an operational mess, and there was no leadership or discipline to be found anywhere!

Functional excellence isn't a dream; it's a necessity. In the three sections in this chapter, I'll outline steps you can take to avoid these kinds of problems and achieve functional excellence within your own organization.

## COURAGEOUS, DISCIPLINED LEADERS

It's not unusual for a company to treat the functional areas, such as finance, information systems, manufacturing, procurement, and HR, as second priority to the business units when it comes to staffing. Hence, you don't always find the highest-quality talent in the key jobs in these areas. This often causes these functional organizations to assume they are subservient to the various line organizations and to management. This is a huge mistake and can lead to suffocating complexity and operational disasters.

Standards of excellence in those functional areas will atrophy with mediocre staffing. Without strong leadership, managers in those areas will likely do anything that the business units or the management tell them to do. What these functional areas should be doing is assuming that the shareholders are their clients, and they should strive for simplicity, efficiency, and effectiveness in the company. If instead they are catering to each and every whim of the various organizations in the company, things will quickly become confused and complicated.

To avoid this mess, these functional areas should sometimes challenge the business units and the management, especially if what they are being asked to do will fragment the overall efforts of the company or put it at risk. And when new technologies are emerging, these functional organizations should be pushing hard to take advantage of them. All of this requires strong, active leadership. Let's take a look at an example involving British Petroleum that demonstrates how incredibly important it is to have tough leaders in the key functional areas of an organization.

John Browne became the CEO of British Petroleum in 1995, and it didn't take long for his strong cost discipline to earn him a very positive reputation on Wall Street. His skill at controlling costs became extremely important when BP purchased Amoco in 1998 for $53 billion and Arco in 1999 for $25 billion. BP needed to achieve huge synergistic savings after these purchases for them to be worthwhile.

During the 2000–2004 period, Browne constantly reminded the troops that "the drive to manage cost and to raise unit margins has become a way of life."[1] The strength of the cost emphasis at BP overwhelmed a lot of the functional leaders within the company whose responsibilities were broader than just cost cutting. The heads of the manufacturing and production facilities also had such responsibilities as safety and maintenance and needed to be sure nothing got in the way of achieving first-class safety and operational and maintenance practices.

By 2005, it was becoming clear that the balance between functional excellence and the drive for cost control was a problem. An anonymous BP employee who had worked at both the Texas City, Texas, refinery and the Prudhoe Bay facility reported that the ongoing mantra was, "Can we cut cost ten percent?"[2] This became such a strong priority that at the Texas City facility, funds for such basic maintenance as painting and external corrosion control were cut so much that leaks started to appear.[3] Employees believed that middle management wasn't taking the situation seriously and had developed an "it-can't-happen-here mentality" toward safety risks.[4] BP was moving managers in and out of facilities very rapidly, and each new boss would attempt to beat the cost efficiencies achieved by the previous holder of the position.[5]

Given this situation, it's not all that surprising that a huge explosion occurred at BP's Texas City refinery facility in 2005. The accident killed fifteen people, injured more than 170, caused a significant disruption in the operation of the facility, and led to a major civil lawsuit on behalf of the victims. The plaintiff's lawyer in the case turned up thousands of damning internal BP documents.[6]

Unfortunately, BP didn't learn from this mistake. The situation got even worse in March 2006 when a BP-operated trans-Alaska oil pipeline in Prudhoe Bay developed a dime-size hole caused by corrosion. This tiny hole caused five thousand barrels of crude oil to spill out onto the Alaskan tundra. The subsequent investigation discovered that a six-mile stretch of this pipeline was badly corroded. After BP shut down the pipe, it was determined that there were twelve spots where 70 percent of the wall had eroded, and there were 187 spots where the wall was 50 percent eroded.[7] This incident led to the loss of hundreds of millions of dollars as well as monumental PR problems for BP. The oil spill was cleaned up, leaving behind a two-acre plot of bare ground, and BP's reputation was badly scarred.

In 2007, CEO Browne was replaced by Tony Hayward, a twenty-five-year veteran of BP at the time. Just before being appointed CEO, Hayward criticized BP, stating, "We have a leadership style that is too directive and doesn't listen sufficiently well."[8] Apparently Hayward was ineffective in changing that style, in that BP was responsible for a huge rig explosion on April 20, 2010, killing eleven people and generating a massive crude oil spill in the Gulf of Mexico.

In investigating this Gulf of Mexico disaster, the U.S. Congress uncovered e-mail showing that before the explosion, when the contractor Halliburton Corporation recommended that twenty-one "centralizers" be used to stabilize the well before cementing it, BP engineers decided to use just six to save BP time and expense.[9] In rejecting the use of the extra centralizers, the BP well team leader, John Guide, commented, "it will take 10 hours to install them.... I do not like this."[10] The U.S. Congress also noted that BP engineers selected the least expensive "long string" method—that is, a single pipe to connect the source of oil on the ocean floor to the bottom of the floating well, in order to "save a good deal of time/money."[11]

The lack of focused, principled, functional leadership to champion the issue of safety within BP could not have been clearer, given the examples of Texas City, Prudhoe Bay, and the Gulf of Mexico. Safety should have been the highest priority for the manufacturing and production organization within BP. In a cost-focused environment, the leader responsible for manufacturing needs to be very strong. A corporation such as BP should never compromise safety or maintenance standards in the face of a cost-control effort. The company needs to be efficient, but much more important, it needs to be safe.

▣ ▣ ▣

BP shows, very clearly, just how critical it is to have incredibly strong leaders in the functional areas. Many organizations hire mediocre talent to fill functional roles, but they should be doing just the opposite.

Here are the characteristics I believe you should look for in personnel who are going to have functional responsibilities in your organization:

- *Tough and stubborn.* You need leaders who don't give in. When they are convinced they are right, they should fight for their cause. The leaders of these functional areas should not budge when it comes to issues that are vitally important for the organization, no matter how hard the management or the business units are pushing back. There should be no compromises in regard to issues like safety, quality, and technical soundness. BP teaches us that you need tough leaders who can withstand tremendous pressures to inappropriately cut corners and cut costs.

- *Principled.* Key functional personnel should have excellent judgment, common sense, and ethics, and need to consistently demonstrate that they work from a sound set of principles. In the finance area, accounting and governance standards should never be compromised. The HR organization should be pushing to design and execute both a world-class performance appraisal process and a system for dealing with poor performers and stretching strong performers. This kind of excellence should be pursued in each of the functional areas.

- *Striving for simplicity in the organization.* Often when the profits are good and revenue is increasing, functional areas tend to increase in size because they believe that they can afford to execute all the various requests for "nice to have" bells and whistles coming from the business units and the management. As I have discussed, this can lead to fragmentation of the organization and excessive bureaucracy and bloating. You need a strong leader to make sure headcount is restrained and only very significant new projects are taken on.

- *Alert to new trends.* Leaders of functional organizations should make sure they are serving shareholders well by properly exploiting new technologies and improved methods that have been proven in the marketplace but are early in their adoption phase. This enables your company to get out in front on important new operational trends. You need strong leaders who are proven change agents and who understand the underlying technologies of their functional area. These leaders bring talented people into their organization so that they are able to spot key trends and take advantage of them.

Although it's true that organizations need a cost-conscious environment, the role of functional leaders is to make sure that all their responsibilities are carried out in a quality manner. You need very strong personalities in those positions if you expect them to exert their authority and resist compromising on important issues. Sometimes compromise can put a company in jeopardy. Clearly BP has learned all this the hard way.

# DISTRIBUTED BUT CENTRALIZED OPERATIONS

For decades there have been arguments about whether to centralize or distribute the talent and responsibilities in functional areas, such as IT, HR, purchasing, finance, and manufacturing. I believe that it is critically important to strike a balance. On the one hand, a company that becomes too decentralized can end up with a variety of approaches to common processes, leading to excess cost and complexity. On the other hand, when functions are too centralized, the personnel lose touch with the needs of the business units and aren't as market driven as they should be.

### A Lack of Balance

I've seen many organizations that have centralized the functional areas of their company far too much. One glaring example was a consumer products company whose centralized purchasing department bought ingredients and chemicals. One of the chemicals was used by three of the operating divisions in very large quantities. The centralized buyers were purchasing it from three major suppliers.

Two of the three suppliers were highly preferred, and the purchasing executives had very close relationships with the executives of those companies. In fact, the relationships were too close, and opportunities were often missed to create more competition among the three suppliers. The operating divisions argued that the company should occasionally take on a new supplier who was emerging in the industry and who might bring new creativity and technology to the manufacturing process and might also provide a competitive cost advantage.

The core problems were that those buyers were left in place far too long and they were too detached from the operating divisions. Further, the performance of these buyers was not regularly appraised, so there was no way to objectively judge their contribution to the company. This sloppiness was the responsibility of the senior VP of purchasing, who had been in his job for fifteen years and had lost all sense of urgency. Eventually the operating divisions convinced the CEO to deal with the stale personnel in the excessively centralized corporate purchasing organization. But over the years, both opportunity and money had been wasted due to this overly centralized approach to purchasing. The key lesson here is that although you do need professional buyers, you also need business unit knowledge and motivation to grow the revenue and profits.

I've also seen many examples of functional areas that were far too distributed and had no centralized coordination or performance criteria. I regularly worked with a food company that was quite global in its product reach, and many of its products used sugar. Unfortunately, each of its operating divisions had its own set of buyers and developed its own relationships with sugar suppliers. There was a surprisingly large difference in the prices that the various divisions were paying for this basic ingredient. Huge opportunities were being wasted. They could have combined their purchasing power to obtain volume discounts.

Also, over time, the personnel in these purchasing positions felt a closer affinity to the operating division than they did to their functional area of purchasing. This often caused them to lose their objectivity regarding the balance between quality and price. They were under constant pressure from the operating division to reduce cost and often would cut corners on quality in order to please.

## The Correct Balance

In both of the examples I've just described, the companies experienced problems because they lacked the correct balance between centralization and distribution of functional resources. Balance can be difficult to achieve, but it is balance, combined with strong leadership, that will make your organization work well. Let's look at two companies who ultimately managed to find that balance.

In 2000, Honda Motor Company was saddled with one of the auto industry's most challenging problems: it planned to convert a manufacturing line designed to produce one model into a line that would produce a different model. At this time, it was common practice in the industry to devote a particular manufacturing line to the production of a particular model. When Honda, for example, launched a new model, it would build a new manufacturing line for that model in Japan and then duplicate it at various sites around the world by converting an old line to make the new model. This was extremely time-consuming and expensive. Introductions of new models were often delayed by years so that automotive companies would have adequate time to build production facilities to make the cars.

Some manufacturers are still using this archaic process in 2010. Ford spent over $75 million as recently as 2008 to overhaul an SUV plant to make one of its smaller models.[12] This reconfiguration process took Ford thirteen months, and the inability to get smaller cars to market more quickly was a lost opportunity for Ford, given the severe recession in 2008–2009.[13]

Honda, however, realized there must be a better way to do things, and in 2000 launched an overall manufacturing plan to utilize robots and to create a global and flexible manufacturing system. This system was designed and developed by Honda's central manufacturing and planning group, but was implemented in manufacturing sites around the world. The intention was to create one standardized way to manufacture vehicles globally. The company was striking an excellent balance, with the central organization doing all the designing, development, and selection of vendors, while the manufacturing sites focused on excellence of execution.

In 2001, Honda began converting its manufacturing lines to utilize robots that could be reprogrammed for different production needs. Honda spent hundreds of millions of dollars to overhaul its manufacturing lines to incorporate world-class robot technology and create flexibility. When beginning to manufacture a new model, some robots were quickly reprogrammed so they would know where to weld; for other robots, "workers simply put different 'hands' on the robots to handle the parts for different vehicles."[14] Manufacturing lines could be reconfigured to produce a new model in minutes.[15]

Honda estimated in 2000 that its savings would be $1 billion per year, but the impact for the company has been far greater than just those efficiency savings.[16] In 2008 when the financial crisis hit, the demand for SUVs dropped quickly and dramatically. As mentioned earlier, Ford was caught off guard and had to spend tens of millions of dollars and over a year to convert its plants to produce small cars; it was estimated that General Motors had to spend $350 million to retool its Lordstown, Ohio, plant so it could produce new models.[17] Honda had a huge advantage. It could make an SUV crossover model at a manufacturing line and within five minutes convert the line to make the very economical Honda Civic model.[18] This led to significant growth in Honda's market share as the economic environment soured in the United States and globally in 2008; it was primarily the result of Honda's ability to quickly switch over its manufacturing lines to make the small cars people wanted.

Honda struck the right balance of centralization and distribution in its key functional areas and reaped the benefits. But not getting that balance right can have punishing consequences. Agilent Technologies is an example of a company that missed the mark and had to work hard to turn things around. I know this case well: I've been on the Agilent Technologies board of directors since 2000.

In 1999, Hewlett-Packard spun off its semiconductor, test and measurement, and medical device businesses to create a new company, Agilent Technologies. The organizational structure of Agilent was fragmented from the beginning. IT personnel in all the various divisions were completely uncoordinated. Also, the company was full of technical people and engineers who loved to experiment with IT systems and computers. These tendencies coupled with a fragmented IT organization created an explosion of information systems, databases, and a variety of different IT tools being used in the company. Agilent's IT efforts in 2000 were neither centralized nor distributed. They were simply chaotic. This led to huge cost inefficiencies.

In 2002, when Agilent began to realize that a major belt tightening within the company was necessary, it was confirmed that 11.4 percent of revenue was being spent on IT systems and activities. That was extraordinarily high in an industry where standard IT spending was about 4 percent of revenue. That spending figure, taken together with the weak financial performance, finally got the problem some serious attention, and by 2005 a full-scale attack on this excess in the IT area was under way.

The new design was clear. The company would operate as "One Agilent": all the key information systems would be handled one way globally and be managed by a small centralized group. There would be no exceptions. It took strong leadership on the part of the CEO and the CIO to make this happen. If either one of those individuals had shown any weakness, the consolidation and efficiency would not have been achieved. Although particular divisions did have some specialized needs, the general argument of "You don't understand—we're different" was simply not tolerated. People were required to make extremely clear and compelling arguments if any exceptions at all were going to be put in place.

The heart of Agilent's business is its world-class test and measurement products and services. This is the source of its competitive advantage. The company's financial systems and processes do nothing to make it more competitive, which means that these systems can easily be centralized—no bells and whistles necessary. Although this change entailed very hard work, the company made significant progress. Fiscal year 2008 ended with Agilent spending 4.2 percent of its revenue on IT, and it reduced that to 3.9 percent in 2009. This put it in a very competitive position in its marketplace—a big change from 2000, when it bore the burden of very excessive IT costs. Finally, Agilent achieved the right balance.

## Balancing Your Organization

As you can see, achieving balance isn't easy, but it can be done. Following are some key principles you can use to strike the ideal balance between the thought leadership and discipline of a centralized operation and the responsiveness and effectiveness of a distributed organization.

- *Manage the key functional fundamentals.* There are three guidelines to follow for managing these key functional areas:

    1. *Create one universal system where possible.* Do things one way across all divisions where you can. If it's an area that doesn't give you competitive advantage, it's probably best to do it one way throughout the entire company. Honda's central development of the robot-intensive, quick-changeover manufacturing line is a good example.

    2. *Only allow exceptions when truly necessary.* If a particular division can really and truly gain advantage by customizing a particular process to meet its unique needs, let that division do so. But beware that everyone has a tendency to claim that he or she has very special needs. Require divisions to present a clear business case for exceptions and hold yourself to extremely tough standards when judging those cases.

    3. *Carefully measure efficiency and effectiveness.* Develop concrete measures and benchmarks for tracking both the effectiveness and the efficiency of the various processes associated with these functional areas.

- *Organize for functional excellence.* For each of your functional areas, such as finance and HR, you need a strong centralized group to make sure that up-to-date, sound technology is being used and that efficiency measures that cut across all the operating divisions are in place. Personnel from functional areas that support an operating division should reside within and be paid for by that division. However, performance appraisals for those functional personnel should be signed by both the leader of the operating division and the appropriate leader within the central group, and both bosses should participate in the actual performance appraisal discussion. That way the person will be told whether or not he or she both served the operating division well and followed the standards and practices the central organization wants implemented. Career management and compensation of the functional personnel within the operating divisions and the functional resources in the central group should be managed by the central functional group. This is to ensure competitive pay for functional people. For a particular industry, an area like finance may be paid better than an area like sales. If the finance person assigned to sales gets paid like a salesman, you could lose the finance person.

- *Assign clear responsibility.* Once you create a strong, centralized group in your organization, you need to ensure that the group's responsibilities are clear. The key responsibility for your centralized functional group is to make sure that both the personnel assigned to each operating division and the personnel in the central group are operating efficiently and effectively. This group should be responsible for evaluating and carefully adopting new technologies and also for protecting the company from getting too far out on the "bleeding edge" of technology. They should be charged with enforcing high-quality measures that gauge whether or not all areas of the company are operating as efficiently and effectively as other organizations within the same industry, if not more so.

# FOCUS ON THE VITAL FEW

Too many active projects and unclear priorities cause slow progress on the things that are actually important in an organization. Unfortunately, managers (particularly managers in functional areas) often don't make the tough decisions to put focus only on the projects that are vital to their company. Failure to properly prioritize can lead to all sorts of problems, the most serious being delays on key projects, as resources are pulled off to staff a variety of far less important efforts.

Let's take a look at a very successful European company whose manufacturing organization didn't provide adequate focus on the most important task, causing some very damaging mistakes.

The giant German drug company Bayer started making its drug Kogenate in 1993 at its plant in Berkeley, California. This drug treats hemophilia and contains a clotting protein called Factor VIII. When Bayer began producing this drug, it could only obtain Factor VIII by extracting it from human blood. But in a later version of this product, called Kogenate FS, the Factor VIII was produced from living cell cultures into which human genes had been inserted.[19] The living cells that Bayer used in this production process came from the kidneys of baby hamsters.[20]

Bayer planned to transition from production of Kogenate to Kogenate FS during summer 2000. The expectation was that there would be a smooth shutdown of the original formula and a quick evolution to the FS version. The FS version of Kogenate was much anticipated in the marketplace because it reduced the possibility of transmitting diseases like the West Nile virus through the human blood products used in the formulation of the original Kogenate.[21]

Consumers were anxiously anticipating the arrival of the new drug. During the first six months of 2000, Bayer was busy building up supplies of the old Kogenate so that it would have an adequate stockpile of the old product while transitioning the facility to create the new product. Unfortunately, priority was placed on building up inventory of the original product, and inadequate attention was paid to the challenges the company would face in making the new version.[22]

As the production engineers at Berkeley were starting to set up the facility for the new process in fall 2000, the FDA showed up for an inspection. What the FDA inspectors found was a fair amount of chaos.[23] Berkeley was in the midst of the transition, and many steps were undocumented or were documented in a sloppy manner. Bayer also completely missed putting the standard FDA audit in its timeline.

The FDA inspection lasted six weeks and caused significant interruptions at the Berkeley plant because key manufacturing personnel needed to provide the inspectors with documents and data on what was happening. By the beginning of 2001, Kogenate FS was up and running, but very sporadically. Because of this, the drug was in short supply, causing physicians and customers to panic. The production levels in early 2001 were about 50 percent of what was needed and originally planned for. Many hemophiliacs were disappointed because they had no alternative but to use the original Kogenate formula.[24]

This foul-up became an extremely emotional issue in early 2001, and by the middle of the year, Bayer executives were apologizing publicly for the shortage. Unfortunately, they still could not estimate how much of the new Kogenate FS they would be making during 2001.[25] Then things got even worse. The FDA issued a report based on its lengthy visit in late 2000, and it blasted Bayer for shortcomings regarding worker training, record keeping, statistical analysis of samples, and more.[26] The FDA indicated that if these problems weren't addressed within a very short period of time, it would consider issuing fines and demanding a plant shutdown.[27]

One of the biggest problems noted in the FDA report was poor quality control. Bayer would receive reports that a particular aspect of the process was moving out of acceptable limits, but there were no procedures in place to catch these trends early and fix them. This resulted in serious emergencies once the problems became bad enough. The crisis atmosphere then generated further problems and delays.

Finally, Bayer's top management realized what a huge mistake it had made in not giving higher priority to the preparation for Kogenate FS production. The top management team of the plant was replaced, and a new team of twenty-five experts from throughout the company was created to turn things around. Bayer also hired numerous quality-control engineers who better understood the process required to manufacture the drug properly, and Bayer's research director for biological products was moved into the Berkeley facility to supervise. It ended up taking eighteen months and costing $30 million to overhaul the Kogenate FS manufacturing operation.

███

There is a powerful lesson here: there is no substitute for extreme focus on vitally important projects. Lack of focus and proper prioritization can lead to far more than just some minor inconveniences.

Here are a few steps you need to take on an ongoing basis to keep your organization's priorities on track:

- *Determine what projects are key to your business.* When deciding what projects should be a priority, you need to make an objective assessment of all options. The key word here is *objective*. The appropriate data need to be assembled and viewpoints need to be heard so that you have all the facts when considering ideas. Patience and thoroughness are critical. The key questions are, Is the idea doable? Is it of high impact? Select only a few of the highest-potential ideas.
- *Put a time limit on the decision making.* In many organizations, the exercise of selecting your best options can take an unacceptable amount of time. Putting structure to this exercise will limit the time the organization takes to cull the ideas. Without structure, people can lose their objectivity, and the discussions can become bureaucratic and emotional.

- *Staff the big one with top people.* Once you've decided which effort is your highest priority, you need your top-performing people to lead the effort. This will not only produce the best possible results but also send a message to the organization that this project is important.

- *Don't assign key projects to already burdened groups.* If a project is a top priority, don't give it to a group or person who already has a lot of work. Treating your most important projects as part of "business as usual" never works. When a group of people have a particular set of responsibilities and are asked to take on an additional project, they are likely to treat that project as second priority. This is true even if the project is positioned as a very high priority for the organization. On key projects, you need to organize separate efforts to make sure they are executed well and achieve the desired results.

- *Review projects regularly and kill what's not working.* Managers find it very difficult to shut down projects. Thorough, regular reviews, at least monthly on key efforts and weekly during crucial periods, will keep you focused on how things are going and force you to assess potential. Be objective. If a project isn't working, change your approach or terminate it.

- *Make it clear to the troops which efforts are key.* You need to communicate broadly to the entire group what the most important priorities are and how the organization is planning to achieve them. This puts proper focus on the key efforts and gives visibility to the people in charge of delivering results. This visibility will put some pressure on the team to yield results and will also serve as a form of recognition for their efforts and successes.

- *Measure progress regularly and report it publicly.* Early in a project's life you need to nail down exactly what the crucial measures are, how they will be reported, and on what schedule.

The success of a business can depend on making key projects top priority and keeping money and staffing from getting tied up in nonessential projects. Bayer failed here. The new drug production should have been given the highest priority and staffed with the best people, but instead the company focused its energy elsewhere, which wound up costing it millions. You need strong functional leaders in your organization who have the courage to put aside low- and medium-priority projects and focus on what's important. Not doing so can be devastating.

# 7

## PRINCIPLE VI

# Create a Culture of Innovation

You don't have to be around a company for very long before you get a sense of the culture. A leader sets the tone in his or her organization. For an organization to be consistently innovative, the leader needs to make it clear that innovation is highly valued: success must be rewarded publicly, and, perhaps even more important, people should not be punished or publicly criticized when an innovation fails.

I spent twenty-six years at Procter & Gamble in a variety of roles. During that period, the company held an annual meeting at its global headquarters in Cincinnati. All its headquarters-based management personnel and the leaders from all the international subsidiaries were invited. Individuals were asked to speak if they had a unique story of innovating a bright idea, making it happen in the marketplace, and having sensational results. The CEO concluded the two-day session by summarizing lessons learned in the past twelve months and the goals and challenges for the future.

I vividly remember how in 1990 a brand manager of Pantene from Taiwan dazzled the audience at the annual meeting with a sensational television ad and a brilliant marketing program that introduced Pantene shampoo and conditioner in that country. Before telling you about the presentation, let me give you some background.

Procter & Gamble acquired Richardson-Vicks in 1985. One brand that was part of that acquisition was a very small department store hair-care product called Pantene. P&G folded this small brand into its hair-care operation, and by 1988 decided to discontinue the brand in department stores. P&G had no expertise in selling to those kinds of retail outlets; its strength was in the large grocery, drug, and mass merchandiser distribution channels. P&G did, however, retain the legal right to use the name Pantene in the future.

The brand manager for Taiwan explained at that annual meeting that they used the marketing slogan "hair so healthy it shines" coupled with a terrific new product formulation that contained vitamins to nourish hair. They brought those two things to life in a TV ad that depicted attractive Asian women with beautiful long black hair. The women spun around, and you could see their hair shine brilliantly. It was breathtaking. The combination of the stunning visual of absolutely gorgeous hair and the sound logic of making hair healthier with vitamins was marvelous. This Taiwanese brand manager was on the stage at the annual meeting because this combination of product and advertising had been an instant success in Taiwan and was taking off in several other P&G subsidiary countries. It looked like Pantene could become the market leader in the hair-care category very quickly.

Taiwan's advertising and marketing plan for Pantene was rolled out globally in the early 1990s, and by 1994, less than four years after its original launch in Taiwan, Pantene was the number one hair-care brand in the world. By 1996, it was in seventy-eight countries; by 1998, it was in ninety countries, with worldwide sales of over $1 billion, thanks to the incredibly innovative marketing strategy and the persuasive advertising developed originally in Taiwan.

So what is the moral of this story? At that annual P&G meeting, everyone was reminded that the most important thing at P&G was coming up with bright ideas that worked in the marketplace and fueled the overall success of the company. In 1996, P&G's vice president and general manager of hair care showed just how committed the company was to innovation. When questioned about the future of Pantene, a product that was already globally dominant, he said "as the global category leader, it would be easy for us to sit back and enjoy our success, but that is not the P&G way. As we move into the next century, we will remain in the vanguard. Our objective, as always, will be to focus our resources to find new and better ways to provide consumers with reasonably priced products that answer key unmet needs."[1] This fundamental message was made clear over and over again throughout the year, not only at an annual meeting.

Leaders must make innovation count. It needs to be a ubiquitous part of the company culture. The three sections in this chapter give some guidelines that will show you how to make this happen in your organization.

## THE CORE VALUE: AVOID COMMODITY HELL

It takes real courage and hard work to consistently, day after day, challenge your organization to be innovative. Once you achieve some sort of success, it is easy to sit back and view the situation as mission accomplished. The secret is getting the people in your organization to understand that the competition is always right around the corner with yet another bright idea that will drive your product to commodity hell, causing you to compete only on price. To avoid that, they need to be constantly coming up with innovative ideas that make your products exciting and distinctive in the marketplace.

Deere and Company has been around a long time, perhaps because the leadership at Deere has always understood that innovation is the key to product superiority. The company, founded in 1837 by John Deere, was the first to sell a steel plow. The plow made the task of tilling the soil significantly easier and more productive. More than 170 years later, Deere is still innovating. For example, in 2006 it developed an eight-wheel tractor that can navigate a field on its own, guided by computers and a global positioning system (GPS) that gets its signals from Deere's own satellite network.[2] The company also developed sensor technology in 2005 that automatically adjusts the loading bucket on construction equipment so that it picks up the largest possible scoop without the operator taking any action at all.[3]

The goal of all innovation at Deere is to make sure the company and the customer both win. Deere front loaders that implement its sensor technology make it easy for a relatively inexperienced operator to do a good job. Companies can pay an inexperienced operator $15 an hour, whereas an experienced operator would cost twice that.[4] This means real savings for Deere's customers. For Deere, such innovations mean better profit margins than its competition and leading products that further solidify its relationship with its customers.

When Robert Lane became CEO of Deere in 2000, the company had great strengths in its brand, dealer organization, products, and loyal employee base. What it didn't have was a great business. Lane's goal was to achieve 12 percent operating return during economic droughts and 28 percent in good times.[5] His plan was to achieve this by continuing to innovate new and better products. His point of view was simple: "You cannot get into commodity hell."[6] Lane fully realized that the only way to sustain strong economic performance is through innovation that will keep you ahead of your competitors.

Over the decades, the majority of Deere's innovation was in mechanization of farming tasks. More recently, the focus has been on automation. One example of automation innovation is a driverless mower for athletic stadiums.[7] Another example is a new cotton-picking machine that is in the final stages of development, which Lane views as a "high-tech intelligent factory on wheels."[8] Current machines have to stop to empty the cotton they've picked every ten or fifteen minutes. But Deere's new model will be able to operate continuously for an estimated twelve straight hours, which is about the time it will run out of gas.[9] Whereas the typical "cotton grower in a developed farm economy like the U.S. needs four to six pieces of support equipment, four to six seasonal laborers, and a $425,000+ machine to bring in his crop, Deere's new two story tall machine enables the grower to harvest even more acres virtually by himself."[10]

Lane makes no apologies for Deere's massive investment in new products, nor should he. His view is that "if you just continue with tired products, pretty soon you can't charge the margins you need. Commodity hell is what happens if we stop investing and we stop delivering."[11]

All of this is paying off handsomely for Lane and Deere. When Lane became CEO in 2000, the stock price had been stuck in the $20 range. By mid-2008, it was in the $70–$80 range. Deere was hit hard in late 2008 by the global recession, but continued to invest heavily in technology to avoid commodity hell.

▣ ▣ ▣

To achieve this level of innovation and subsequent financial success in your organization, you need to create a culture that nurtures innovation. Here are some key tips that will help you and your organization stay constantly out in front:

- *Communicate your goal of innovation, regularly and thoroughly.* Your goal is to constantly innovate new and better products and services. The easiest way to make people understand that this is a critical company value is to tell them. Whether with quarterly messages, casual conversations, messages to the outside media, or all these things, you need to make your goal clear—all the time.
- *Encourage and inspire innovation.* A good leader lets the innovators know they are appreciated and that they have the leader's confidence. You can do this with surprise visits to the innovator's office just to chat and give encouragement, mentions of innovators' work in both large and small meetings and through regular communication devices, and small notes of encouragement sent occasionally. P&G inspired innovations by holding an annual meeting to herald recent innovations. It doesn't matter how you do it; the point is to let the innovators know you respect and believe in them.
- *Reward innovation.* When an innovation effort is complete, be it a success or not, the leader needs to reward the innovators. This can be done with a special recognition lunch, a forty-five-minute chat in the innovator's office or your office, or a meeting with a high-level executive that you've arranged to thank and encourage the innovators. Use your imagination to come up with fresh new ways to simply say thanks to your innovators and to make it clear

that you appreciate them. My view is that emotional rewards are more appreciated than any kind of financial reward would be.

- *Instill a sense of urgency in the troops.* It's important to convey a sense of urgency at all times to the organization. You need to use all the usual tools—monthly or biweekly reviews, a critical path schedule, and status reports. It also helps just to drop in to the offices of the key players occasionally and tell them the effort is important and ask what you can do to help. Maintaining urgency is toughest after you have achieved a particular goal. Success causes people to sit back and relax. You need to be relentless in your push for yet another bright idea to drive those products and services to yet new levels.
- *Never get into a price battle.* If a battle with the competition is focused completely on price, you have failed to create a product or service with exciting and unique advantages. It's better to abandon or sell off a particular business if, over a reasonable period of time, you simply have not been able to get out of the trap of a price battle. It says that you're bringing nothing special to the party.

There is nothing more dreadful in business than to market a product that is just not distinctive in any way, leaving you no option but to battle it out with the competition on price. As Deere's Robert Lane says, avoid commodity hell! Innovate!

## CREATIVITY AND SIX SIGMA DON'T MIX

Innovation is not an orderly process. People who are good at it tend to go through many ideas before coming up with one that works. It's also a very fragile process. A manager can stifle innovation without even knowing it through his or her spoken or unspoken communications. People who are charged with innovation are constantly observing how their management is acting and reacting. Unfortunately, they often interpret their management's behavior and casual comments as specific instructions or constraints that need to be followed.

Over the last decade, process improvement techniques such as Six Sigma have been given a lot of publicity. Six Sigma is rigorous and disciplined methodology that uses data and statistical analysis to measure various aspects of an organization's operational performance, thus raising questions and suggestion areas for possible improvement. Its main use is to take variability out of a process, reduce errors or defects, and increase the predictability of a process. Some leaders grab hold of Six Sigma and attempt to apply it everywhere within their company. This tends to be a big mistake, considering that innovation is such a fragile and variable process; by definition, Six Sigma is a tool for taking the variability out of processes.

Few companies have been given more accolades in the area of innovation than 3M. 3M invented masking tape, Thinsulate, and Post-it Notes. Unfortunately, by the late 1990s, life had become quite challenging for the company. "Profit and sales growth were wildly erratic," according to *Business Week*. "It bungled operations in Asia amid the 1998 financial crisis there. The stock sat out the entire late 1990s boom. The flexibility and lack of structure, which had enabled the company's success, had also by then produced a bloated staff and inefficient work flow."[12]

In December 2000, wanting to turn things around, 3M announced that Jim McNerney of General Electric was stepping in as the new CEO. Considering that GE was both an early adopter of Six Sigma and one of its strongest proponents, it was not surprising that he brought along intense interest in implementing Six Sigma at 3M.

McNerney could hardly have pursued Six Sigma with more gusto. Soon after his arrival, thousands of 3M employees were being trained as Six Sigma black belts, which qualifies them to be used as consultants within the company. Virtually every employee in the company was given extensive "green belt" training on how to use data, create charts, and minimize variability and errors in what they did.[13]

Because 3M had been suffering in the late 1990s from too much emphasis on creativity and minimal structures concerning how things were run, McNerney enjoyed almost instant success. Because the main value of Six Sigma tends to be to drive out cost and save money, McNerney had a lot of opportunities, and "in his first full year, he slashed capital expenditures 22 percent."[14] He held R&D funding constant for four years, hovering at just over $1 billion per year. In a move that was viewed as highly suspicious by employees, McNerney revised the way that R&D work was done to shape it into a process. In the past, researchers at 3M had been given very wide latitude in their pursuit of innovation. When the Six Sigma process was applied to R&D, it reduced that latitude and was seriously questioned by the researchers. Steven Boyd, a researcher who worked at 3M a total of thirty-two years, commented that the questions generated by Six Sigma "are all wonderful considerations, but are they appropriate for somebody who is just trying to . . . develop some ideas?"[15] Applying Six Sigma to the R&D processes at 3M led to more predictable, incremental improvements in current products, but kept researchers from focusing on bold new innovations.[16]

There is no doubt that McNerney's heavy focus on process improvement had a positive impact in his first few years at 3M, given the rather chaotic state of the company when he came on board. But after that, innovation stalled, and so did the business. The stock price moved from $60 in December 2000 to a high of $90 in June 2004. Then the lack of 3M innovation began to take its toll; the stock declined in McNerney's last twelve months and was $72 in July 2005 when McNerney departed to become the CEO of Boeing. During his time as CEO, McNerney had reduced the number of employees by 11 percent (eight thousand workers), put in place a tough performance review process, significantly reduced capital spending, and utilized Six Sigma to drive out cost and variability; during his reign, profits grew an average of 22 percent a year, but clearly, creativity was down.[17]

When McNerney left the company, the entire 3M organization agreed that they had lost their creative edge.[18] Although historically the company's goal had been to have one-third of its revenue each year come from new products released into the marketplace, in the five years that McNerney was CEO, that percentage dropped to 25 percent.

McNerney was replaced by George Buckley, a veteran 3M employee. For the majority of Buckley's career at 3M, employees were not only allowed to hunt around for internal funding for a pet project but also were encouraged to spend 15 percent of their time on independent projects, which sounds very much like the Google environment of today. Traditionally, the culture at 3M allowed for a lot more risk, and tolerated failure quite well. Of course, those were the traits that got the company into trouble in the late 1990s.

Buckley was convinced that Six Sigma had a legitimate role in improving processes, so he left Six Sigma in place in the process-oriented operational parts of the company. However, he also realized that it was just the kind of tool that could sap the innovative capabilities of an organization. He noted soon after he took the job that "invention is by its very nature a disorderly process. You can't put a Six Sigma process into that area and say, well, I'm getting behind on invention, so I am going to schedule myself for three good ideas on Wednesday and two on Friday. That's not how creativity works."[19] Buckley quickly tackled the issue of innovation at 3M by restoring a lot of the proven 3M practices of the past, and eliminating Six Sigma from areas where innovation is the priority; in essence, he acted on his understanding that innovation and Six Sigma don't mix.[20]

Much has been written about 3M concerning innovation. For many of 3M's most successful products, years of testing were required. Probably its most famous product, Post-it Notes, took about five years of experimentation before the product finally went into the marketplace in 1980.[21] One twenty-seven-year researcher at 3M, Michael Mucci, who was subsequently dismissed from the company in 2004 as part of McNerney's downsizing, commented, "We all came to the conclusion that there was no way in the world that anything like a Post-it Note would ever emerge from this new system" because this long period of experimentation wouldn't have been allowed under Six Sigma.[22]

The lesson from 3M is very clear: you need a balanced effort of process improvement and innovation to be successful; you can't overdose on either one of them. In the late 1990s, the focus on efficiency and process improvement was minimal at 3M, and the company got in financial trouble. During McNerney's tenure, the pendulum swung the other way, and creativity and innovation dropped as process improvement took priority. Six Sigma works well in improving processes because you don't want them to vary; you want them to be precise and consistent. But Six Sigma does not fit well when you are trying to innovate, because innovation calls for variation and needs to allow room for failure and surprise.

▨ ▨ ▨

There are valuable lessons here on the issues of proper use of process improvement techniques and protecting the very fragile innovation capabilities of your organization. The ideal path is to strike a balance between these two very different and important aspects of running a company. So how do you put yourself on this path? Here are a few guidelines that I believe will help:

- *Communicate clearly that you value both.* You need to make sure your organization understands that you put a high priority on improving processes but that you also put a high priority on innovation, making sure that it is not subjected to excessive discipline and measurement. Your people need to clearly understand that you want both process improvement and innovation, but not together.
- *Apply process improvement to processes, not creativity.* Enthusiasm for Six Sigma and similar tools can quickly get out of hand, and process improvement can begin to take over the whole company, as it did at 3M. Your company can benefit from such tools as Six Sigma, but you must make sure the organization realizes when and where they should be used (that is, to improve processes).
- *Unleash your innovators, but be clear about constraints.* Creative individuals tend to be fairly fragile. They often worry a lot about whether or not management thinks their ideas and projects are worthwhile. Hence, you need to ensure that they understand that their job is

to innovate, not second-guess what high-level bosses want. They shouldn't be concerned with others in the company who may have other agendas. However, if you're looking for results in a particular area, you need to set parameters and constraints and communicate them clearly. Lack of clarity about limits can lead to innovation shutting down due to lack of focus or to the pursuit of bizarre ideas that waste the organization's time and money.

- *Don't play favorites.* It is very easy to look as though you're playing favorites without even realizing it. If you are constantly giving credit to profit-oriented short-term projects, which often happens with process tools like Six Sigma, and never patting innovators on the head publicly, it's very clear what kind of behavior is being encouraged. The reverse is true as well: excess focus on creativity with no hard-core revenue and profit goals for the overall organization sends the wrong message. Be sure you praise and reward both types of efforts equally.

There is no doubt that such tools as Six Sigma are powerful in reducing variability in important processes that you use to run the company. But remember, for areas of the company where you are counting on innovation and creative ideas to drive revenue and customer excitement, you need to avoid process thinking and encourage an environment of risk-taking—with the appropriate focus on getting ideas to the marketplace.

## REWARD FRESH THINKING

It's not easy to create a culture where people feel free to innovate and truly believe that innovation is not only welcomed but necessary for the livelihood of the organization. Leaders can unwittingly generate fear of failure with a few slips of the tongue, and word gets out quickly. To avoid this sort of confusion, you must clearly reward fresh thinking, especially when it generates results.

In the previous section, I discussed how 3M has been a remarkably creative machine over the hundred-plus years of its existence. So what has this company done, over the years, to inspire fresh thinking?

3M's rewards system is a crucial element in its success with innovation. One way that 3M has rewarded its employees is by celebrating each year the people who have achieved outstanding innovation. Hundreds of such employees are singled out through an employee voting system and given high-profile recognition.[23] This takes the form of articles in company publications, all-hands meetings focused on celebrating the winners, and inexpensive but treasured mementos. In addition, 3M selects twenty of its truly outstanding innovators each year and sends them and their spouses on a four-day holiday at 3M's expense.[24] The trip is not only a treat for the selected employees and their families but also a highly visible honor, which is just as important.

These rewards are soundly based in reality; 3M does a great job of measuring the impact of innovations that emerge. Each year, the company carefully measures the amount of revenue that is coming from products that were introduced recently (the past four years) to judge the overall productivity of its R&D efforts. This measure lends credibility, because people know that finance has verified the revenue impact, and the external world is being told about it. This documented impact gives even more prestige to the recognition the innovators receive.

There's no doubt that 3M represents a superb example of properly rewarding fresh thinking. In contrast, the household appliance giant Whirlpool has had difficulty with rewards. Although Whirlpool also has done some very creative things over the years to encourage innovation, it has struggled with whether or not to pay employees for innovative ideas. Following several years of debate on this subject, Whirlpool's rewards system evolved so that a third of the senior leaders' pay is related to results coming out of their innovation pipeline—or, said another way, one-third of their pay can decrease or disappear, depending on their innovation results. The company leadership believes that this approach was critically important in changing the mind-set of management, enabling them to truly internalize the desire to be world class in innovation. However, people at Whirlpool don't get paid for bright ideas. Instead, the individuals who play a lead role in generating successful innovation become renowned within the company. As Nancy Snyder, Whirlpool's director of strategy development, noted, "The reward is recognition by your peers."[25]

These examples from 3M and Whirlpool can give you a sense of the range of effective ways to reward fresh thinking, which is a vital component in achieving a culture of innovation.

The following are some guidelines for establishing in your own company a culture that clearly supports and highly values innovation:

- *Define success: excellence in execution and fresh ideas.* Before you can reward your employees for success, you need to define what success is and what you expect from people. First, they need to execute their current job with excellence. Second, the company highly values new ideas in regard to all aspects of the business. Creative thinking is incredibly important to every organization, but other job responsibilities can't fall by the wayside in pursuit of innovation. Managers must properly communicate the importance of both objectives.
- *Only reward innovations that have measurable impact.* A leader needs to constantly communicate that bright ideas alone are not enough: they must have an impact. In regard to products and services that are provided to customers, this impact can come in the form of incremental revenue, increased market share, and a variety of other marketplace measures. In regard to improving internal processes, the impact is typically cost reduction or various efficiency and productivity improvements. It's your job as the leader to set the expectation that an innovation is only as good as the concrete impact it has on the organization's performance, and to set rewards accordingly.

- *Provide emotional rewards.* Many organizations have found that the most productive way to reward individuals for fresh thinking is through public acknowledgment. Such recognition lets the individual's peers know that the creative ideas were of value to the company and provides the person responsible with some fame. The P&G annual meeting, which I described in the introduction to this chapter, is an example of a very effective way of celebrating innovators' achievements. Emotional rewards also go far in establishing a culture that reinforces the importance of a constant flow of new ideas.

- *Make executive compensation innovation dependent.* Many companies have had success basing a portion of executive compensation on the percentage of revenue generated by new or improved products or services. This is especially effective if executives are managing large divisions or several divisions. For executives managing functional areas, compensation can be partially related to efficiency and effectiveness improvement. Such approaches to compensation are valuable ways to encourage executives to carry the message that innovation is highly valued to their troops. Naturally, you can also get creative on this front and consider bonuses for an entire group based on the group's ability to innovate. There are all kinds of ways to slice this, but one thing I've learned over the years is that it can be destructive at the middle and lower levels of the organization to give monetary rewards to individuals for ideas. However, it can be quite valuable to provide monetary rewards to the whole organization and to the executives running key components of the organization for achieving significant impact through valuable innovation.

Probably the key lesson regarding the task of creating a culture of innovation is that there aren't just one or two things that make this happen. You are trying to create a mind-set, not just intermittent bursts of creativity. You need to communicate the importance of innovation regularly and in numerous ways.

# 8

## PRINCIPLE VII

# Demand Accountability and Decisiveness; Avoid Consensus

C reating a climate within your organization that fosters excellence in innovation is not easy. Too many organizations experience long periods with no significant innovation. Often this is due to the complicated way decisions are made. The people you are counting on to innovate need to know that the buck stops with them; they are accountable to generate meaningful innovation. They also need to know that there is a sense of urgency, that they need to get on with things. They need to be decisive and not rely on teams, task forces, committees, or other consensus-oriented vehicles, which encourage compromise and eliminate distinctiveness, a key element of innovative ideas. Let's take a look at an example that is full of decision-making pitfalls.

I once worked with a software firm that developed and marketed systems to help small companies execute their business. The software ranged from inventory management tools to a package of basic accounting modules, which was the firm's core product. There was a department manager who was in charge of all these different software products, maintaining them and developing new features to attract new customers.

As the sales personnel of this firm worked with customers in selling and supporting this software, a lot of suggestions naturally would emerge regarding additional features or performance issues that customers wanted the vendor to address in its next version. Such input can be great fodder for innovation.

In maintaining the various software products and developing new innovative features, this department manager organized his people into groups: technical architecture, user interface, and database management. Each of these groups had about twenty people organized in a variety of different ways.

As suggestions came in from sales, they would be directed to the department manager, who would forward these various suggestions to whichever of the three groups seemed appropriate. One of the problems here was that no single person was held responsible for each product. To make changes required help and consensus from all these groups. Also, the selected group leader would forward the suggestions to a unit within his group that already had specific responsibilities. This meant that the suggestion was given second priority. The way the organization was configured made it very difficult to implement a new innovative idea that would excite customers.

This organizational structure emerged at the very early stages of the company's life. When the firm had only one product, the basic accounting package, it made sense to have a group of people working on the architecture, a group assigned to deal with the user interface, and another group dealing with the database methodology, with an overall leader being accountable for the product and for integrating those capabilities in order to excite the customer. But as this company grew and launched products in other areas, the organization did not evolve so as to easily incorporate innovation. For each product, nobody was uniquely accountable for its success; the structure forced consensus decision making and virtually prohibited decisiveness.

You run into these kinds of problems in organizations all the time. The remainder of this chapter outlines some guidelines that will help you avoid such situations. The guidelines will significantly increase your organization's ability to achieve the kind of innovation excellence you need in order to remain competitive.

# SET CLEAR ACCOUNTABILITY, GOALS, AND MEASURES FOR INNOVATION

Innovation is often viewed as incompatible with things like accountability, goals, and measures. This is just not true. When you are pursuing innovation, accountability is necessary to keep the innovators focused. It is another common misconception that really innovative individuals simply can't be managed; you just have to hope that some brilliant ideas will pop out. The role of a leader is to select the person who will be accountable and then excite that individual about the dream—that is, the area where innovation is desired and the impact it will have. The more concise the leader can be about the dream, the better. It focuses the innovator and leads to the obvious and necessary discussion about specific goals and measures. When creating a system of accountability, however, you need to emphasize with the person accountable the pitfalls of consensus management. New products, product features, or processes typically affect a lot of people in the organization, so there will be a lot of input. Requiring a consensus from all the people involved or affected would kill the innovation; it would strip away the unique and distinctive aspects that make the idea innovative.

The best system I've ever seen for setting clear accountability, goals, and measures was in place while I was working at Procter & Gamble from 1968 to 1994. Each brand at P&G was assigned a brand group. The group consisted of anywhere from three to seven people including the brand manager. Typically, that brand manager might have as little as four years' experience with the company or as much as six. In the brand group, the junior people would be referred to as brand assistants, and those more senior would be assistant brand managers. Two or three administrative assistants would likely be assigned to the group to help with the administrative tasks.

The role of the brand group and the brand manager at P&G was to advocate for their specific brand. No one else reported to this group, and they provided the leadership in the company in making things happen for that brand. They were responsible for the revenue and market share of this brand as well as the profitability. Their job was to generate the product and marketing innovations that would cause their market share to grow. An important but second priority was making their profit targets. It was a very focused goal, and the accountability was absolutely clear.

Each year at P&G, about a third of the marketing people would be let go. There was an extremely detailed and carefully executed performance appraisal system that made it clear to poor performers that their time at the company was limited if they didn't tackle their weaknesses. It was definitely an up-or-out system, and the top management of P&G was using marketing to ferret out the very best talent in growing these consumer brands. In fact, the majority of the top management at P&G is traditionally from the brand management area of the company.

The R&D, product development, and manufacturing people were assigned to specific brands, but reported up through their own chain of command; they did not work for the brand group. Also, there were other supporting groups, such as finance and HR, that had resources assigned to handle the needs of the brand groups, but again, they did not report to the brand group. The power of the brand group was that it had almost a direct communication link to the top management of the company regarding all issues of that brand. If manufacturing was causing the brand group problems in getting a bright idea to the marketplace, it was the brand manager's job to escalate the problem. Similarly, if product development was going too slowly in a particular area that the brand group believed could have a big impact in the marketplace, it was fair game for the brand group to make it clear to the top management of product development and the top management of the company that either things needed to improve or they needed different resources to make the progress they believed should be made in these areas.

Because of their role, the brand management personnel at P&G were often viewed as a pushy bunch of people who were always in a hurry. Frankly, that was by design. They knew they were being held accountable and that their careers were on the line if they didn't get results. Clearly, they were highly motivated to get their brand's market share moving along and to get those profits up to the desired level.

The measurements for the brand groups were very obvious. We've already mentioned market share and profitability. They also had great market research resources available, enabling them to perform various studies that would show how a particular product compared to the competition, from both a technical and a consumer perception standpoint. There were also good marketplace measures on the habits and practices in particular categories of business as well as terrific measures of the impact of advertising.

The simplicity of this organizational design is striking. It's all about clear accountability, goals, and measures. It makes P&G feel like a very small company because each brand is basically run by a small group of people with a lot of supporting groups, working to make things happen in the marketplace. It's a terrific design. Although it has been refined modestly over the decades, the core notion of the brand manager being *the* advocate of the brand has been a powerful organizational approach that has proven the test of time.

Let's take a look at a major automobile company that took the opposite approach, with devastating results. Instead of the clear accountability that P&G had in place, Ford Motor Company used a system of consensus management when designing and releasing products into the marketplace.

Ford had a very difficult time during the 2000–2009 period. In 2000 the stock price was in the $25–$30 range, but during the decade it steadily declined. In mid-2009, it sat at $7.50, due to continuing problems and the financial crisis. Although much has been written about the punishing labor contracts and retiree pension programs, one of the key problems at Ford during this period was the lackluster automobiles it offered its customers.

When Ford hired Alan Mulally away from Boeing to be CEO in fall 2006, it didn't take him long to spot that one of Ford's major problems was consensus management in the process of designing automobiles. Soon after joining Ford, Mulally became very frustrated when he found that the Ford Fusion, a sedan launched in early 2006, didn't have a navigation system, satellite radio, or side air bags. All its competitors had this type of equipment, even the lower-priced Hyundai Elantra.[1] When Mulally investigated why, he learned that there was no one person responsible for the innovation and design of a vehicle; and, due to a policy requiring consensus among all departments, the finance department at Ford was able to request that those items not be standard equipment in order to get the car's price down.[2]

The same problem occurred on the Ford Escape, where the stability control system was left off because the finance department wouldn't concur.[3] This had big implications in the marketplace. *Consumer Reports* did not include the Ford Escape on its recommended list primarily because it had no stability control system. Unfortunately for Ford, that *Consumer Reports* recommendation list is highly persuasive with car buyers.[4] Mulally decided that there had to be a recasting of the role of finance at Ford, and the roles of any other groups who were compromising innovative impact. Mulally summarized his overall assessment with a simple but important statement: "There's been no accountability."[5]

Probably the most damaging example of consensus management at Ford was in the area of design. Management should have given responsibility for design and innovation of each vehicle to one person, just as P&G gave responsibility for a brand to one person. Fortunately for Ford, Mulally went after these accountability problems very aggressively, and by 2010 Ford was clearly outperforming GM and Chrysler (both went into bankruptcy) and actually survived the financial crisis fairly well. By late spring 2010, the stock price had climbed back to the $13 range, and it was gaining market share.

The fundamental lesson here is clear: consensus management doesn't work when the task is to generate exciting innovation that will have a big impact. Leaders need to protect their innovators from such decision-making practices.

Although I am sure that many brilliant ideas have emerged without structure and accountability and even from companies requiring consensus management, putting some degree of focus around the task of innovating really improves the overall productivity of the effort. Here are some guidelines that I have seen work well in companies to generate fresh thinking and new ideas that can really pay off:

- *Put one person in charge.* Any group that is assigned the task of innovating needs one leader who is accountable for the group's progress. He or she needs to be held responsible for avoiding the kind of consensus management that can destroy good ideas.
- *Find strong-willed, senior talent for the job.* The task of managing the group charged with innovation should never be assigned to junior staff. It should be given to experienced and proven talent. The person you pick for this job should give his or her staff strong guidance, but also the freedom to do their jobs.

  You need individuals who are not only very innovative but also somewhat stubborn, so that they will persevere when they hit roadblocks, such as claims that the idea is too costly or difficult to implement, or that it is "too unique" to be successful. They need to be tough, to push back hard, and to fight for what they believe is right.
- *Create focus.* You need to carefully define what innovative success looks like so that you get the results you want and can measure them. The work of innovation often leads in surprising new directions. This can be fantastic, or it can waste a tremendous amount of time and money. You need an experienced leader to give the innovation process focus and to constantly remind the group of the innovation goal. Your leader must also have the courage to kill ideas that are too far removed from the area of focus, and the ability to maintain high morale among the people in the group.
- *Agree on measures up front.* At the start of the innovation search, you can save a lot of time by giving adequate attention to the issue of how things will be measured. These measures can take

a variety of forms. Maybe it's a head-to-head blind product test against your competitor. Possibly it's the technical performance of the innovation itself. No doubt there are instances where measures just aren't possible, but wherever you can, find a way to measure success. Agreeing to those measures before you start work will also give your team a clearer idea of what they are working toward.

• *Keep the focus on impact, not internal politics.* Many people in the orga-nization will believe that anything they say should immediately be honored and acted upon. The leader of the innovation process needs to train his or her innovators to focus first and foremost on the customer impact of what they are doing. If the product is being modified to increase its appeal, the focus needs to be on the customer's seeing a big difference and the modification's generating a big business impact. If the innovation concerns an internal process, the focus should be on the efficiency and effective-ness gains. Don't waste time in endless internal meetings arguing politics because the organization fears change. Again, single-person accountability can avoid time wasted in meetings where everyone wants a say.

• *Challenge outside input.* Much of people's input regarding new ideas and improvements is good and can be implemented sensibly, but certainly not all of it. Sorting out which input is useful and which is just designed to protect some person or organization from change is vital to success. You need to make it clear that all input, no matter what level or organization it is coming from, will be challenged concerning its credibility.

When you are after innovation, you want to avoid hordes of people who are organized in a sloppy manner and potentially competing with one another. Nothing beats clear accountability, goals, and measures to ensure that people take the responsibility seriously, and what can be clearer than one person driving change forward? When the majority rules, no one has accountability, goals get overlooked, and bright ideas become ordinary.

# BE DECISIVE—KILL MARGINAL PROJECTS QUICKLY

In pursuing innovation, keeping too many ideas alive decreases your chances of finding a terrific idea and deriving the maximum impact from it. What happens typically is that ideas emerge and quickly spawn projects. Many organizations have no real process for deciding whether to staff these projects or put them aside, so what begins as someone's pet project soon becomes institutionalized. Although the person heading the project may get regularly questioned about its eventual impact, the ever-growing group working on it and its leader become more and more attached to the effort and defensive about putting it aside. As the effort drags on, showing only average potential, it gets more than its fair share of management attention, which saps energy that should be placed on the ideas that clearly have potential. All of this wastes time and money, and dilutes your efforts. Strong leaders are decisive; they don't allow marginal efforts to drag on. You have to regularly review the portfolio of projects being pursued and close down the low- and medium-impact efforts. That takes courage.

Tyco is one organization that got itself into a real mess because it lacked focus and had too many different projects and products soaking up its resources. When Ed Breen took over as CEO of Tyco in summer 2002, the challenges were enormous. The credibility of the company had been ravaged by scandals generated by the prior CEO, Dennis Kozlowski.[6] It had $11 billion in debt coming due in 2003, and the company needed a completely new board of directors because the prior board had lost all its credibility.

During the Kozlowski era, a large number of very different businesses had been accumulated. The company seemed to value the number of businesses it acquired more than their financial impact. There were more than two thousand legal entities that made up the company, and they sold a perplexing variety of products, such as electrical security systems, diapers, metal conduits, industrial valves, pharmaceuticals, sprinkler systems, printed circuit boards, and medical imaging equipment. Breen faced a huge challenge. He had to clean up the marginal projects and businesses and restore some basic credibility to Tyco. He also had to convince Wall Street and shareholders that the company had a sensible plan and was recovering.

Early in his tenure, after a thorough review of all existing businesses and their potential, Breen decided that Tyco's new strategy would be to tightly focus on fire protection, security, and engineered products, such as valves and pipes for handling very hot oil and gas. This was a very decisive and important step made quickly so that the company could regain some focus. Breen's goal was for Tyco to be an industry leader in each of those three areas. He then set out to implement his plan and pare down the company, closing down or selling off the off-strategy efforts.

By late 2004, Breen had terminated or divested all the businesses that were viewed as marginal. In total, over half of Tyco's businesses were sold off, due to their nonstrategic nature or their weak performance.[7] By early 2006, all this consolidation was really paying off. The company had avoided a liquidity crisis, and debt had been reduced from $28 billion in 2002 to $10 billion in 2006.[8] In this period, Tyco's stock price moved from $8 per share up to $36.

In June 2007, Tyco sold off its health care division as well as its electronics unit. This left Tyco where it wanted to be: focused on fire protection, security, and its industrial valve business.[9] The resulting company was extremely healthy, with cash flow of $800 million in 2007 and a substantial recurring revenue stream from businesses that had strong continuity with their customers and required relatively low amounts of capital investment.[10] Also, because the company didn't require a whole lot of R&D, Tyco's R&D budget had been reduced to only $120 million, only about 0.6 percent of sales.[11]

Breen did a magnificent job saving the company. He was very decisive. He selected a clear strategy, terminated or sold businesses that made no sense, and killed nonstrategic or marginal projects to end up with a highly focused and well-running business. Ideally, of course, it's best not to get into a situation that requires the company to be saved. Target is a company that historically has had a superb process for quickly dealing with off-strategy and marginal projects to prevents its getting into those sorts of situations in the first place.

One of the most admired retailers in the world, Target is in the top fifty on the Fortune 500 list. This sort of success is impressive given that it regularly goes head-to-head against powerhouse retailers like Walmart.[12] Target's revenues were almost $65 billion in 2008 and had increased at an annual rate of 12 percent during the 1998–2007 period.[13]

One of the core competencies of this organization is its unique positioning in the marketplace. The strategy that it attempts to live up to with each and every item available in the store, as well as with the look and feel of the store itself, is "expect more, pay less."[14]

Given Target's financial track record and its success in achieving a very clear image in the marketplace, it's pretty obvious that this company has done a great job in killing off-strategy and marginal projects. The one individual most responsible for that is Michael Francis, the head of marketing. Francis has spent his entire career at the retailer. "Every single thing that Target's logo appears on—from the donation of $1,000 to an elementary school to the look of its private label garbage bags—goes through Francis. His job is to immediately kill anything that is going to violate, in his estimation, the sacred logo of Target of 'expect more, pay less.' "[15] He is assisted in this task by his very talented marketing division, and he gains incredible insight into what is going on in the marketplace through Target's unique "creative cabinet."

The members of the creative cabinet are a highly valued group composed of about twelve people of various ages, interests, and nationalities. They are handpicked by Francis personally and rotated regularly so that they don't get stale. The objective here is fresh perspective on what's happening in the marketplace and what seems to be popular with consumers. Members of this cabinet are paid annual retainers to file reports on their observations and have conversations with Francis about them. The group never gets together. Francis wants to avoid any kind of "group think" as he collects information on how products in the marketplace are being received by consumers.[16]

Using this creative cabinet as a source of ongoing information, along with the insights he gets from his staff, Francis personally says yes or no to proposals on what items should be stocked in Target retail outlets. He doesn't hesitate to terminate an idea immediately at the outset if it violates the model of the company. Also, if mistakes have been made and items are simply not moving, it is his job to quickly put them aside in favor of new items.

It's amazing to see an over $60 billion retailer operating like a very small organization, quickly deciding yes or no on whether to stock an item and basing those decisions on a very systematic but open process for collecting key information.

Francis and Target have been immensely successful at what they do. From 1994 to early 2008, Target's operating margins have moved from 5.4 percent to 8.6 percent, whereas those of Walmart have decreased from 8.1 percent to 7.3 percent.[17] Stockholders have also been treated well, with a return of 795 percent, compared to 284 percent for the S&P retail index and 354 percent for Walmart.[18] The "expect more, pay less" strategy along with decisive decision making that kills off-strategy items and marginal efforts have clearly paid huge dividends for this retailer.

Tyco and Target offer robust examples of the need to constantly review new ideas and the value of assessing existing projects, products, and businesses to make sure they are consistent with the overall strategy of the organization and are contributing at or above expectations. Most important, both companies teach us the power of decisiveness in putting aside marginal efforts.

Here are a few guidelines to help you ensure that you are following these companies' example in your organization:

• *Set clear goals with significant impact.* Doing this may sound simple, but far too many organizations don't set clear goals. Instead they add projects here and there, with the intent of eventually focusing and sorting everything out. To improve your chances of generating meaningful innovation, you need a clearly stated and specific goal that, if achieved, will generate very significant impact. That goal may relate to the products and services of your company or the improvement of an internal process.

- *Have a rigorous process for evaluating projects.* You need to create a data-driven organization that is highly objective. As a leader, you can create that kind of value system by exhibiting those characteristics yourself as well as demanding them of all of those in key decision-making roles in the organization. Too often leaders in an organization become frustrated at its lack of ability to come up with great ideas, so they'll accept an idea and staff it, even though minimal supporting evidence exists, just to get to the next step of doing something. Don't let this happen. Have a process in place to evaluate projects, and allow only great ideas to move forward. Michael Francis plays the decisive role of judge and jury at Target, and he demands big impact.

- *Monitor projects closely.* A real weakness in many managers as they pursue innovation is their lack of follow-up; they fail to regularly check on the status of projects or to decide whether or not the effort should be terminated or continued. Without some level of monitoring, projects can get off track, or efforts that might not be achieving the original goal can continue. Once again, the tough leader will make sure that a rigorous process is in place to monitor projects.

- *Leaders, not committees, should be the decision makers.* You need to avoid group decision making that depends on the agreement of numerous parties. Decisions by consensus let everyone off the hook because no one is responsible for investigating the facts and doing the hard thinking. The person in charge of a project needs to know that the buck stops with her and that her career is on the line.

It takes courageous leadership to kill projects that people are attached to. Keeping marginal projects from surfacing in the first place can be even more difficult and requires systems to be in place to control whether or not a project will be granted life. But difficult as these actions may be, they are absolutely essential in driving innovation. Decisiveness and high standards are key attributes of great leaders.

# 9

## PRINCIPLE VIII

# Exploit Inflection Points

Significant shifts in the technology or the consumer habits and practices underpinning your industry are often referred to as inflection points. They are very important because they can cause the existing products or services in the industry to be rendered inferior, out-of-date, or old fashioned. To take advantage of inflection points and to keep from becoming obsolete, you must either replace your current offerings with up-to-date new products or modify your existing products. There are many examples of the importance of inflection points. Let's review a few.

In the 1990s, a major inflection point in the photography industry was the emergence of digital photography. It was becoming apparent that it would revolutionize the industry. Kodak, one of the biggest players, had people working on digital photography in several different areas of the company, but none of them seemed to be aware of the others. It was shocking when, given the dominance of Kodak for decades, it was Sony and Canon that launched the early entries (mid-1990s) into the emerging digital camera category. Their products quickly gained consumer attention. I suspect no company had more people working on digital photography than Kodak, but they had little to show for their effort.

By the late 1990s and early 2000s, digital photography became the rage, and digital camera sales were growing 30 to 50 percent per year. Kodak was nowhere to be found. Although it did launch some digital cameras that were respectable in their performance, Kodak was always late to market and could not keep up with the rapid pace of technology improvements being introduced in the marketplace by Canon and several Asian vendors on almost a monthly basis.

This story has a sad ending. It's not clear whether Kodak will survive. It is currently pursuing a line of printer products to generate some revenue, but it's a company that absolutely lost its way because it missed a key inflection point.

On a more mundane front, let's discuss liquid laundry detergents. In the 1970s and early 1980s, Unilever had the leading liquid detergent, called Wisk. At the time, liquid detergent formulas weren't as effective as powder formulas, and Procter & Gamble's powder detergent Tide (called Areal in Europe) had a much larger market share. Liquid detergents really didn't become a major factor during this period because, after a few uses, consumers recognized that they were inferior cleaners.

P&G realized that there were convenience advantages to a liquid detergent and knew that if a liquid detergent ever matched the cleaning power of powders, it would probably take over the category. Hence, P&G had been working for years to come up with such a formula, and eventually its scientists emerged with a product test that showed success. It was a new liquid formulation that matched the cleaning power of Tide powder. Given that R&D had clear technical evidence that this new liquid formulation was hugely superior in cleaning power to the existing liquid detergents that were on the market, and fully equivalent to Tide powder, the Tide brand group knew that this new liquid formula would be a major inflection point in the detergent industry. The brand group submitted a proposal to management recommending that the new liquid formulation of Tide be launched and marketed alongside Tide powder.

The CEO of the company pushed back very hard because Tide had such a strong reputation as a superior cleaning detergent. He wanted to be totally convinced that the new liquid formulation matched the cleaning power of Tide powder and that customers would still be satisfied after extended use of the new liquid.

Many additional consumer tests were performed, and all the data confirmed that the new formula met the objective. These data finally convinced the CEO. It was clear that P&G chemists had generated a significant inflection point in the detergent industry. P&G launched Tide liquid with advertising that focused on the fact that consumers could now get the superior cleaning power of Tide in whichever form they preferred, powder or liquid. The Tide liquid formula revolutionized the detergent business and was a gigantic inflection point that P&G worked hard to achieve and then exploit.

A third example relates to portable music. Sony invented the category in the late 1980s with the Walkman, which initially played cassette tapes and, later, CDs. This product dominated the portable music category throughout the 1990s, but in the latter part of that decade, a digital music service called Napster emerged on the Internet that allowed users to swap digital music. The format of the digital music as it is loaded onto a PC from a CD is called MP3 and can be easily sent over the Internet or loaded onto small portable digital music devices called MP3 players. These small digital music players allowed people to listen to music in a very convenient way. The problem was that swapping music over the Internet was illegal. Consequently, portable MP3 players were not a big idea at that point.

Nevertheless, Sony clearly should have been looking at the technology and realizing that someone was going to figure out how to make all of this legal and capitalize on it. Unfortunately, Sony simply couldn't get out in front of that inflection point—but, to the surprise of everyone, Apple did. The iPod was introduced in fall 2001 and wiped out the Sony Walkman. Steve Jobs and Apple had jumped all over an important inflection point, and Sony had missed it completely.

What do we make of all these stories? To achieve innovative excellence, you must spot inflection points early and develop products and services that will enable you to lead the charge. The rest of this chapter will provide some very important guidelines that, if followed, should enable you to spot and create inflection points and become a leader in your industry.

## STAFF WITH EXPERIENCED, CUSTOMER-FOCUSED LEADERS

The talent you assign to spotting and exploiting emerging inflection points is critically important, particularly the leader of the effort. You increase your chances of innovation success if you select individuals to lead the effort who are confident following their instincts, developed through varied prior experience. Also, the individual needs to have a deep respect for and curiosity about the customer, and the belief that exciting the customer is the only thing that counts.

If you don't have the right people concentrating on making the most of emerging technology and trends, your company can miss important opportunities. Let's take a look at a Japanese company that had a fantastic chance to make a splash in the global marketplace but didn't have the right people with the right knowledge to seize the opportunity.

NTT DoCoMo is a very large wireless phone company in Japan; it serves over fifty million customers and has a reputation for always being on the leading edge of technology. For example, it was a leading-edge innovator in the area of wireless Internet standards.[1] Given its excellent batting average for coming up with exciting new applications way ahead of the rest of the global market, DoCoMo would have been the logical company to emerge as a global powerhouse in the mobile wireless area.

In fact, it set out to become such a global leader back in 2000 and 2001. DoCoMo had a very exciting wireless Internet service for mobile phones called i-mode. I-mode was one of the first products to offer Internet access on a mobile device. Cell phones with DoCoMo i-mode were all the rage in Japan. One particularly popular i-mode application was instant messaging. Teenage girls in Japan loved it. They would send literally hundreds of short messages to their friends each day. DoCoMo's i-mode wireless Internet protocol was so ahead of its time that many people thought it would emerge as the global standard. Unfortunately for DoCoMo, this didn't happen.[2] DoCoMo made expansion of i-mode into Europe a high priority, but after several years of effort, it had only three million customers out of Europe's 450 million cell phone users.[3] Its failure proved quite damaging financially. In 2004, DoCoMo suffered a 29 percent drop in operating profit and a 4 percent decline in revenue. That was DoCoMo's first ever fall in operating profit and revenue.[4]

DoCoMo's core problem was simply inadequate sensitivity to other cultures and to consumer habits in other countries. As *Newsweek International* said, "DoCoMo managers were so enraptured with their state-of-the-art service that they failed to notice that the long and intricate menus favored by Japanese consumers were not well received by foreign customers who were looking for more direct and intuitive interfaces."[5] The entire senior management team was Japanese, and this hindered DoCoMo significantly when trying to appeal to other markets.[6]

This DoCoMo example is reminiscent of numerous failures by the Japanese when dealing with technology innovation. The problem is certainly not a lack of technological prowess. In fact, Japan spends more on R&D as a percentage of GDP than the United States. They also register significantly more patents than any other country, including the United States. As noted in *Newsweek International*, the core issue for the Japanese is that "while Japanese companies like DoCoMo, NEC, Sony and the like struggle with incremental improvement, competitors like Apple and Google are fusing innovative technology with great marketing, design and distribution to create entirely new product categories."[7] To do that requires personnel who are highly talented in numerous areas and have extensive and varied experience. Personnel also need to be very creative and able to take recent consumer trends and the latest technology and fuse them in highly innovative ways. This requires an environment where bureaucracy is at a minimum and risk-taking and failure are not issues—one very unlike the Japanese industrial environment.

Many people blame the lack of cross-industry innovation coming out of Japan on the traditional hierarchal corporate structures that exist in its big technological powerhouses. Business analyst Christian Caryl observed, "Japan Inc. still remains dominated by big, vertically integrated dinosaurs with little maneuverability and a marked disinclination to creativity. The strict hierarchies of Japanese companies discourage people with radical new ideas."[8]

Japanese companies are notorious for having strict boundaries between groups within the company. This is one of the reasons why a company such as Sony would have such a difficult time inventing the iPod. Its software skills resided in the PC division, its hardware skills were in the consumer electronics division, and its music division, although successful, operated independently within Sony. Obviously a product like the iPod required tight integration of all these capabilities blended into a single offering. This kind of creation means that a company has not only to ignore internal boundaries but to exploit them.

▨ ▨ ▨

Assembling the right group of people to keep your organization on the cutting edge of technology isn't easy. Making sure they have the space and resources they need to do their jobs well is no easier. Here are some characteristics to look for when putting your team together and some guidelines for keeping them productive:

- *Assemble a strong team.* You need to be very disciplined in assembling any group of people who you are hoping will be highly creative and innovative. And a group of individuals operating on the cutting edge of technology needs to be as broad based as possible, representing highly varied skills and interests. Some things you should look for when assembling your team are
    - ○ *Breadth of experience.* The people you assign to this task should be highly experienced in a variety of different areas of your organization. They need to be confident enough to jump into

a new situation and quickly figure out what's important and where the opportunities reside. Usually these traits are not found in people who have spent large amounts of time in one area of the organization., You want people who have worked in multiple areas and maybe even multiple companies.

o   *Total commitment to consumers.* Total commitment to understanding and pleasing consumers is absolutely necessary. Ideally, the people on your team should have extensive experience sorting through consumer data and spotting trends. They should also be very comfortable with any technologies involved, and have a real talent for exploiting technology to achieve consumer benefits.

o   *Intelligent risk-taking.* It's important that individuals doing this kind of work believe in their instincts, take risks based on those instincts, and have a proven track record. They also need to be able to absorb new information and to change direction or modify their thinking about a particular trend or consumer behavior based on that information.

•   *Don't encumber creativity with bureaucracy.* The worst thing you can do to people who are charged with finding and exploiting inflection points is put them in a bureaucratic environment. If they have to cut through a lot of red tape or get lots of people to concur with what they are doing, they'll end up spending most of their time compromising and scheduling meetings. That's not how you want these talented individuals to use their time.

•   *Keep the group very small.* Strong performers know how to get work done and don't like to be encumbered with an excess of people. Also, involving too many people dilutes responsibilities and creativity.

Your most important decision in identifying and exploiting inflection points is in your selection of talent. Following the tips I've just outlined should improve your chances of success in this area.

## BE FIRST

When one company, brand, or product is consistently first to the marketplace with new ideas and features, customers notice. If their experience is good, that company will usually emerge as their preference, which is a huge psychological and business edge for the victor. But being first isn't important only when it comes to the products and services being offered to customers. It also applies to the processes companies employ internally to achieve efficiency and effectiveness. You want leaders in your functional areas consistently to be the first to point out and exploit new approaches to your processes that will give you the edge over competitors.

Very few companies understand the importance of being the first to bring new ideas to the marketplace better than Schlumberger. This company was founded in 1926 by two brothers, Conrad and Marcel Schlumberger, and is still based on their innovative techniques that use electrical currents to locate hidden pockets of oil deep underground. Schlumberger doesn't own oil fields, and it doesn't own the oil that it helps get out of the ground; what it brings to the party is deep expertise on how to find the oil and then extract it.

In recent years, Schlumberger has consistently come up with industry-leading ideas and techniques for guiding drill bits through miles of the earth's surface to find oil. It has industry-leading techniques in seismic imaging, which uses sound waves to map the structure below the surface of the area being investigated. It also has been first at what is referred to as "well logging." This consists of lowering an instrument that has numerous sensors down into a well to determine details of the rock structure along the drill hole. Sadad Husseini, a former executive vice president of Saudi Aramco, Saudi Arabia's national oil company, indicated that Saudi Aramco's work "would be very hard to do without Schlumberger. Schlumberger has been critical for Saudi oil field development."[9] This shows how being first and being best can affect your relationships with your customers.

Schlumberger has also been the first to understand how the balance of power has been shifting in oil production. The company took note of Russia's emergence as a national force in oil exploration. As Russia acquired premier assets from the likes of Royal Dutch Shell and BP, Schlumberger was right there to assist the Russian government in developing capabilities to get the oil out of these big fields in Siberia and on Sakhalin Island.[10] Today, Schlumberger has fourteen thousand employees in Russia, and its revenues there topped $1.5 billion in 2007, triple its revenues of 2004.[11] Understanding the evolution of state-owned petroleum reserves and being first to assist such national companies as Saudi Aramco, Mexico's Petroleos Mexicanos, Gazprom and Rosneft in Russia, and a dozen others have definitely placed Schlumberger in a clear leadership role in the oil production industry. These national companies now control more than four-fifths of the known oil reserves in the world.[12]

Schlumberger deserves a lot of credit for what it did back in the late 1990s regarding R&D. During the period when oil prices dropped to just over $10 a barrel, many of the large oil companies, such as Shell and Exxon, cut back on R&D.[13] Schlumberger did not. Instead, it developed new and very efficient ways of extracting oil and gas from the earth, which positioned it as a leader when the oil industry became healthy.[14] Even in 2008–2009, when other major oil companies were spending about 1 percent of their revenue on R&D, Schlumberger spent 3 percent.[15]

Schlumberger's integrated project management (IPM) unit is yet another example of how aggressive this company is in coming up with new ideas that enable it to be first in the marketplace. IPM offers the customer the opportunity to use Schlumberger not only as a supplier of techniques, equipment, and processes to find oil and get it out of the ground but also as a provider of management skills for the actual drilling and ongoing well production. Schlumberger was the first company to provide this broad spectrum of capabilities, all integrated through its proven practices. IPM was developed based on expertise that Schlumberger accumulated while managing important drilling programs and ongoing production for large oil companies and the national oil companies. This was a new area of business for Schlumberger, but one it was very well qualified to enter, considering that it knew the oil production business so well. The rationale for going in this direction was very clear, as explained by Andrew Gould, Schlumberger's CEO: "What you see is more and more people who don't have technical knowledge buying into oil fields."[16] Gould and IPM took full advantage of this trend and offered these newcomers deep expertise in managing a drilling program and managing production. Between 1999 and 2007, IPM's revenue increased fourfold to some $1.6 billion. The current backlog for this unit of Schlumberger is $4.8 billion.[17] Clearly the company had a hot new service on its hands because it had spotted an important trend.

The relationship between Schlumberger and the national oil companies is truly impressive. Partnering with these national companies also enabled Schlumberger to become a much more active global player in the development of new oil and gas projects. Russia's Rosneft unit recently won rights to explore a large field in Algeria, but it had virtually no experience in that country. Working closely with a Schlumberger IPM team, Rosneft was able to launch an effort to begin drilling in Algeria. Drawing on the full set of services IPM has to offer, Rosneft had the IPM team build an airstrip, line up and take delivery of the drilling equipment, and start up production. The effort got off to a great start. Schlumberger drilled two exploratory wells, and both ended up being highly productive for Rosneft. What's new here is that Schlumberger is the first to develop and offer such a full spectrum of integrated services in these new geographical areas. Rosneft simply couldn't do it without Schlumberger. Schlumberger is winning because it is first in developing these new capabilities that are highly valuable to its customers.

Schlumberger's efforts always to be first in developing new capabilities for the oil and gas industry continue to yield huge payoffs. Its reputation enabled the company to land a huge piece of new business in Saudi Arabia. The new Shaybah field in Saudi Arabia has an estimated sixteen billion barrels of oil, but it is trapped in an unusual type of limestone rock, and currently, techniques really don't exist for easily getting it out.[18] However, Saudi Arabia had complete confidence that Schlumberger's deep research expertise would enable the company to solve that problem and awarded Schlumberger a huge contract to partner with the government in its $24 billion plan to boost oil production by 25 percent in Saudi Arabia.[19] At the time of this writing, Schlumberger's researchers are working hard to develop new techniques so that they can be as productive for Saudi Arabia in the future as they have been in the past. It's Schlumberger's strong reputation for delivering state-of-the-art approaches that won it the business, and it is confident that it can deliver again on this new need that Saudi Arabia has placed before it.

■ ■ ■.

As Schlumberger shows, the benefits of being first, and of having the reputation that goes along with that, are huge. But being first takes an enormous amount of work. Here are some of the key guidelines leaders must keep in mind in order for their organizations to be constantly out in front with bright new ideas:

- *Be paranoid about inflection points.* At all times, you must assume that a competitor is right around the corner and that it has spotted and is about to exploit an inflection point that will do big damage to your business. Time is of the essence. You need to spot trends and technologies quickly and jump on them before your competitor does. You need a culture of paranoia.
- *Make "being first" part of the culture.* Create a culture that takes pride in constantly being first in spotting and exploiting key trends and new technologies. To achieve this, you must continually remind your troops that they need to come up with smart new ways to run the organization and please customers. Showcase examples of doing this well and communicate this goal repeatedly in meetings and documents.

- *Encourage early experimentation.* Smart, experienced innovators need to be encouraged to experiment early and often with new ideas. Experimentation is the only way to come up with the next big thing. Chasing a competitor who is beating you to the market with innovation is no fun.
- *Don't discipline curiosity.* It's not the number of people that are important; it's the quality of the talent. Outstanding innovators sometimes have unorthodox ways of drilling into technology or consumer habits to produce unique and valuable insights. As a leader you must have a deep respect for the curiosity it takes to create these results. Creative people are often a bit different in their work habits. Don't be too disciplined with innovators. They should not be told how to do the work; they should simply be told the objective.
- *Don't let projects drag on.* There is nothing worse than being part of a project that seems just to drag on and on. When that occurs, it's a clear signal that you need new leadership or that your objectives are not clear or reasonable (or both). Don't wait too long to replace talent or change direction based on up-to-date learning.

For leaders to excel, it's vital for them to understand the importance of constantly being first in presenting new approaches and new ideas to their customers. Schlumberger is the giant in its industry because it does understand this well and acts on it. The company's leaders are experienced and customer driven, and they strive always to be first with the new idea.

# 10

## PRINCIPLE IX

# Value Ideas from Anywhere

One thing that is certainly true about innovation is that you can't program it. Bright ideas can emerge from just about anywhere. It's tough to know exactly what background and characteristics enable a person to generate valuable ideas. The practical implication of this truth is that you must be open minded to encourage and consider ideas from anywhere—not just from your product development staff but from all employees, consumers, industry analysts, universities, and so on. You need to make sure that within your organization, processes are set up to receive input from the outside and properly evaluate it.

One thing that seems to be true in the pursuit of innovation is that the closer you are to the actual use of a product, service, or process, the greater your chances are of observing or experiencing something that might generate a new idea or insight that brings a new capability or big improvement.

There is a great story in the steel industry related to this concept of careful observation. Back in the 1960s, the steel business in the United States was dominated by large integrated mills, such as U.S. Steel. In 1966, U.S. Steel had an employee by the name of Ken Burns.[1] Burns, a financial guy whose career in the company was skyrocketing, surprised his management in 1966 when he told them he was going to spend his two weeks of vacation in Japan visiting several Japanese steel mills. His management at U.S. Steel thought this was very strange. They believed that because the steel industry in the United States was clearly the global leader, Burns was wasting his time visiting steel mills in Japan.

During his vacation, Burns observed that the steel production process in Japan was far ahead of the United States and had a 30 percent unit-cost advantage. The Japanese had a superior basic oxygen process for making steel and a highly efficient continuous casting process that skipped the typical intermediate step of making steel ingots and then reheating the ingots to make the actual steel products.[2]

Burns came back from his vacation and attempted to tell the key execs at U.S. Steel what he saw and how Japanese technology could potentially be utilized at the company. Being the financial guy, he saw tremendous advantages and several ways for U.S. Steel to get way out in front of its competition.[3]

The management of U.S. Steel heard Burns out, but paid absolutely no attention to what he said. They were confident that the people at their manufacturing facilities were on top of important changes in the industry because after all, they were the market leaders.[4]

As they say, the rest is history. It didn't take long for some very creative people to start up a new steel operation at Nucor. This company consisted of a number of small steel mills, called mini-mills. They capitalized on new low-capacity but highly efficient electric arc furnaces and the kind of continuous casting that Burns saw in Japan. They used scrap steel as their raw material instead of iron ore, and they were nonunion facilities. Each of these mini-mills was a small (by U.S. Steel standards) regional manufacturing plant serving local geographies to avoid high shipping costs.[5]

Nucor revolutionized the steel industry, and the traditional big steel companies suffered accordingly. In fact, Nucor and a few other mini-mill operators drove most of the big steel companies into bankruptcy.[6]

You just never know where a bright idea is going to come from. As the U.S. Steel story suggests, even someone from finance can have a brilliant idea regarding your core processes and products. Consider all ideas, regardless of where they come from. The tips in this chapter will, I hope, provide the right kind of focus to enable your organization to do a better job of turning up and taking seriously ideas from a variety of sources as you strive to become innovative leaders.

## VISIT AND OBSERVE YOUR CUSTOMERS

Turning up terrific new ideas for products and services is vital to a company's growth and survival. Without fresh ideas, your products and processes become inferior to those of your competition. Although it is important to have the latest technology or science to improve your products, it's equally important to understand your customers' likes, dislikes, habits, and practices to know if they're interested in those improvements. You need to understand your customers' experiences. You are trying to spot opportunities that often even the consumer can't articulate.

IDEO is a company that makes a living helping organizations watch and understand their customers. It was formed in 1991 and quickly developed a very strong reputation for being particularly talented at helping organizations tap into consumer attitudes and needs.[7]

When Kaiser Permanente, a very large health maintenance organization in the United States, was trying to increase its patient population and cut costs in 2003, it hired IDEO to help. One thing that was particularly worrisome to Kaiser was that its facilities were rather old and, in some cases, needed significant updates. In the health care industry, updating facilities is incredibly expensive, and Kaiser's leaders thought that the best plan would be to launch a series of new facilities with state-of-the-art capabilities and equipment. Kaiser wanted IDEO to give the company ideas regarding what capabilities its new facilities should have to make them as attractive as possible to Kaiser's customers.[8]

When Kaiser explained its issues to IDEO, IDEO responded that there was an important first step to be taken: IDEO staff, along with a cross section of personnel from the hospital, needed to gain some in-depth insights into customer reaction to Kaiser services as they were currently being offered. On the Kaiser side, this project involved representatives from all the roles in the hospital: nurses, administrative personnel, physicians, and so on. IDEO contributed designers, architects, social scientists, and engineers. This very diverse team designed a whole variety of ways to observe patients who were experiencing Kaiser's services.[9]

The team came up with some startling observations. Kaiser was causing its patients and the patients' friends and family members a fair amount of frustration because the check-in process was difficult and the waiting rooms were unsatisfactory. IDEO also pointed out that although most patients came in with a relative or friend, the process at Kaiser quickly separated the two, allowing few opportunities to interact. This left patients anxious and without any emotional assistance and the friends and family feeling unnecessary and frustrated because they couldn't help and weren't kept informed. In addition, people were assigned to examination rooms and then left alone for long periods of time before medical assistance arrived.[10]

After observing these problems for some time, the Kaiser-IDEO team began to realize that the issue was neither the age of Kaiser's facilities nor the status of the equipment; it was all about the customer experience. IDEO then made numerous suggestions for improving the check-in process, the examination process, and a whole variety of other steps that patients go through, to make the experience a whole lot more pleasant. These changes actually cost Kaiser very little in capital; rather, they entailed changing the process patients went through and realizing that these processes go a long way in forming a customer's overall experience.[11] Adam Nemer of Kaiser summarized it well: "IDEO showed us that we are designing human experiences, not buildings."[12]

The Kaiser experience is typical of the kind of contributions IDEO makes. IDEO now operates globally, and its client list includes some of the most prestigious companies in the world. It has helped many companies design new products or revitalize existing products through its award-winning design services. Virtually all those designs were based on consumer insights gained because IDEO forced clients to actually come in contact with the customers and what they were experiencing. What's amazing is that it requires an organization like IDEO to get some of these big, successful companies to realize they need to go out and talk to their customers.[13] That almost sounds silly until you realize how insulated organizations tend to become. What we all need to realize is that over time, we often make organizations so complicated that getting things done internally becomes a herculean task, leaving no time for such fundamental questions as "How do customers like our product?" and "What can we learn about improving the product by watching customers use it?"

Tesco, a fabulously successful grocery retailer with roots in the United Kingdom, is a brilliant example of a company that closely observes customer behavior and has been very successful because of it. In the United Kingdom, Tesco overcame the giant J. Sainsbury and emerged eventually as twice Sainsbury's size. It then moved into other countries in Europe and Asia and became a $91 billion retailer in the process. Much of its success is due to its painstaking attention to consumer research.[14]

Before Tesco initiated its retailing effort in Japan in 2003, representatives of the company spent three years studying the habits of Japanese families. In fact, many Tesco staff members actually lived with Japanese families in order to make their observations. They learned quickly that there's not much space in a Japanese home and consequently, Japanese consumers don't buy large sizes, don't keep large inventories, and go to retail outlets very often. On the basis of this research, Tesco retail outlets in Japan focused on small sizes, and they were highly successful. In contrast, Carrefour shut down its Japanese operation two years after Tesco entered Japan. Both Walmart and Carrefour discontinued operations in South Korea, whereas Tesco has done quite well.[15] Clearly its success is due to its willingness at the outset to study consumers carefully, watch how they operate in their homes, and learn what their habits and buying trends are day in and day out.

In 2005, Tesco initiated its effort to develop a strategy to break into the U.S. market. The very fact that it planned to come to the United States surprised many in the retail industry. Sainsbury had big difficulties when it purchased Shaw Supermarkets in the United States and eventually abandoned the effort. Marks & Spencer and Dixons also unsuccessfully tried the U.S. market.[16] Mark Palmer, a British business professor, noted, "Analysts refer to the U.S. as the graveyard for British retailers."[17]

So how did Tesco develop a plan? It carefully watched consumers. Market researchers from Tesco lived in sixty California family homes for two weeks, constantly going through their refrigerators and cupboards and shopping and cooking with them. They kept detailed diaries of everything that went on.[18] When, on the basis of this research, Tesco came up with a store it believed would be successful, it actually built a prototype in a warehouse in Los Angeles and invited groups of consumers to come in to shop. Tesco observers watched intently and asked many questions to make sure they understood why shoppers did what they did and what they liked and disliked.[19]

The stores Tesco finally launched in the United States are called Fresh and Easy Neighborhood Markets. The stores are relatively small, about ten thousand square feet, which is about 20 percent of the space of your typical U.S. suburban supermarket. The consumer they target is highly interested in picking up prepackaged, ready-to-eat food, so Tesco stocks prepackaged sandwiches for lunch, and for dinner, they offer healthy alternatives, such as salmon filet, spinach salads, and the like. Tesco's target consumers do not have a lot of extra time to cook but want high-quality food and are willing to pay the price. They are also interested in healthy foods, so Fresh and Easy Neighborhood Markets stock a lot of organic and trans-fat-free items.[20]

Tesco's conclusion from all its research in the United States was very clear: Americans lead very busy lives, leaving little time for shopping and preparing meals, but they still want a quality food experience.[21] Another thing that Tesco has learned about the United States is that different neighborhoods vary significantly in their interests. Researchers found that the Spanish-speaking communities in such states as California and Arizona have different wants and needs than other neighborhoods just a few miles away, and Tesco varies its offerings accordingly.[22]

The secret to Tesco's success is very clear: the company has perfected the art of watching customers very, very closely and understanding in detail what they do and why they do it. Its marketing people also actually visit with customers and have a direct dialogue instead of getting their information through some outside professional market researcher.

These are terrific lessons from IDEO, Kaiser Permanente, and Tesco regarding the power of observing customers very closely. Stepping back from these examples, here are some key points for you to keep in mind to turn up ideas that are just as successful:

- *Get ideas from your customers.* As an organization matures and has some experience with success, too often it becomes internally focused or technology focused. Studying and understand consumers can be seen as a low priority. Your job is to make sure your people charged with innovation are getting out of the office and spending quality time observing and talking to customers.
- *Don't rely solely on quantitative market research.* This type of research is quite valuable in understanding how consumers perceive and react to your products and to the competition. It's also good for tracking trends over time regarding industry habits and practices. But consumers simply aren't going to go out of their way to answer questions you don't ask. Nor will they tell you things that they themselves can't articulate. They may be able to express their frustrations in using a class of products, but they typically can't suggest features that may address those frustrations and be of high appeal. Chances are, consumers didn't know they wanted cup holders in cars before it was an option. Now it has become such a rage in automobiles that it can be a key decision-making point

when buying a car. Before the age of cup holders, I can assure you that no quantitative research had much chance of uncovering that opportunity.

- *Avoid qualitative research.* Qualitative research, such as focus groups and one-on-one interviews, are generally too intrusive. Most focus groups are not trustworthy because you don't know if one particular participant intimidated the rest of the group or even if the interviewer biased the conversation. The same holds true in regard to one-on-one interviews done by a professional researcher. You just don't know how comfortable that consumer was in expressing his or her views or, again, if the researcher was biased.

Strong leaders know that there is no substitute for observing how customers are using their products. Although unstructured activities with customers may test your patience, they are more useful and provide more insight into developing your products and services than any amount of market research can.

## DON'T JUST FOCUS ON YOUR R&D STAFF

Keeping your products and services exciting and dynamic is critical, and too often organizations look only to their R&D staffs to come up with the fresh new insight to keep the business moving ahead. You need to make it clear to all your employees that they have a responsibility to be on the lookout, internally and externally, for fresh ideas that can generate a positive business impact.

Let's take a look at a company that's a source of valuable stories of getting ideas from a variety of different places rather than focusing just on R&D.

Back in 1999, David Whitman, chairman and CEO of Whirlpool, was on a mission to make Whirlpool number one in innovation. Realizing that all his employees used the kinds of products that Whirlpool produced—namely, dishwashers, refrigerators, washers, and dryers—he decided to collect ideas about making these products more exciting from all sixty-one thousand employees of Whirlpool.[23] He put Nancy Snyder, the director of strategy development, in charge of the project.

After some false starts, Snyder created a site on the company intranet and enlisted all employees to submit their ideas. Innovation became the responsibility of all Whirlpool employees, not just R&D. Thousands of people were providing suggestions.[24] Snyder also chose 240 employees to be "innovation consultants" whose job was to review all the suggestions, grab hold of the best ideas, and lead the efforts to get them into market testing.[25]

To avoid a budgeting problem with so many suggestions coming forward, the CEO at Whirlpool directed each of the business units to set up a seed fund for innovation. For the North American unit, that budget was $5 million.[26] When Whitman established these budgets, he told his regional managers, "I want you to fund all of the ideas that come forward. I don't want you turning down any ideas. And if you turn them down, I'm going to tell them to come to me."[27] Those are the kinds of statements that clearly help create the kind of culture that is absolutely critical in focusing the organization on innovation.

In 2005, five years after the employee suggestion program was launched, the effort generated the following new products that were achieving marketplace success: the Gladiator line of cabinets and appliances for the garage; the super-capacity Cabrio line of washers and dryers; and a portable device called the Fabric Freshener, which takes wrinkles and odors out of suits and other dry-clean-only clothing by steaming and air-drying them.[28] Also in 2005, Whirlpool's profits were at an all-time high of $422 million on record sales of $14.3 billion, sending its share price to an all-time high.[29] At that time, Whirlpool valued its innovation pipeline at $3.3 billion, up from $2.0 billion a year earlier, and $1.3 billion two years earlier.[30] There's no doubt that looking outside R&D spawned impressive results for Whirlpool.

Another example of reaching outside your R&D organization to generate fresh, innovative ideas comes from the pharmaceutical industry. Finding blockbuster drugs is becoming extremely difficult and requires a lot of money, years of research, and the evaluation of tens of thousands of chemical compounds, just to find one that has promise. In 2000, Ge Li founded a company named WuXi, focused on a new area of science called combinatorial chemistry, which provides a fast and very efficient method for screening millions of possibilities and discovering preliminary leads that have the potential to become new drug candidates.[31] Given the rapidly increasing quantity of well-educated technical talent, Li set up the company in his home country of China. He offers the services to large pharmaceutical and biotech companies throughout the world.

Giants like Pfizer and Merck quickly jumped on this opportunity to acquire experience, and, they hoped, some good leads from the new and innovative combinatorial chemistry approach that WuXi offered, and by late 2007, WuXi achieved an annual sales rate of $130 million, generating profit of $30 million.[32] This rapid growth is not surprising, given that aggressive pharmacological companies are always looking outside their own R&D groups to turn up promising innovation.

□▤▣

Here are some battle-tested tips that will help your organization think outside the box when it comes to who is doing your innovating. Remember, the more people you have thinking about innovations, the better your chances are of running across that exciting idea that will drive your competitors crazy.

- *Beware of the technology focus of R&D.* R&D plays a valuable role in a company. But the fact is, people who reside in R&D are usually focused on the science and technology of their industry. This approach will sometimes give birth to a great idea, but trying to figure out unarticulated consumer needs and tapping into ideas outside the company are usually not top priorities for R&D folks. You need to think through your organizational design to make sure that you aren't just studying technology and failing to look outward.

- *Drive innovation from outside and above R&D.* It is a big mistake for an organization to assume that innovation is the job of R&D. Somebody outside R&D or above R&D must take on the responsibility for uncovering and nurturing bright ideas that excite consumers. We saw previously in this book that at P&G, the brand manager was charged with finding innovation, with no constraints at all concerning where the idea comes from. At a minimum, the division manager or VP of the division responsible for a particular product needs either to be the driver of innovation or to appoint one from outside R&D.

- *Look everywhere for ideas.* As I've discussed elsewhere, encourage all members of your organization to be constantly on the lookout for bright ideas to revitalize your products and services, create new products, or improve the processes used to run the business. If you compartmentalize your organization, your people will become focused only on their own departments. You want employees to feel responsible for the business and to understand that bright ideas can come from anywhere. We saw from the Whirlpool, IDEO, and WuXi examples in this chapter that good starting points are employees, customers, and companies that provide innovative new capabilities for uncovering ideas.

A strong leader doesn't make the mistake of assuming that innovative ideas come only from R&D scientists and engineers toiling in their labs. You need to create a culture where all employees, including R&D, look outside at customer habits and needs, new technologies, and any other vehicles that can generate new ideas to improve products and services.

## BEWARE OF JOINT VENTURES AND PARTNERSHIPS

The logic of joint ventures and partnerships often seems flawless. Each party brings certain skills to the table that the other does not have. The executives become convinced that the synergy between the two organizations will be terrific, so they go ahead and set up the operation with the anticipation that both organizations will profit or benefit.

Although I'm sure there are some good examples of joint ventures and partnerships working well, there are a multitude of examples where the results are quite disappointing. Some reasons for this are that oftentimes organizations will not allocate their top talent to a joint venture because they want that talent for their own pursuits, not those pursuits in which they have only a half interest. The same hesitancy is sometimes seen in allocating capital for the venture. And all too often the cultures of the two organizations eventually clash.

In many cases, when the going gets tough, one of the two organizations needs to play the lead role in dictating a new direction, but what you often see instead is endless debate that leads to delays, compromises, and numerous headaches. The joint venture or partnership itself begins to suffer because of dissention, weak morale, and lack of responsiveness to the needs of the marketplace.

If you sense that I am fundamentally negative about joint ventures and partnerships, you're right. Odds are that they won't be as successful as all parties dream they can be. Let's take a look at a couple of examples that demonstrate some of the problems.

In late 2007, Dow Chemical announced a joint venture with Petrochemicals Industries (PIC) of the State of Kuwait. Dow would contribute its commodity chemicals assets and expertise; Kuwait would bring the availability of very low cost oil and natural gas—the key raw materials used in making these commodity chemicals. The problem that Dow was tackling was that its commodity chemicals business was highly dependent on oil and natural gas; in buying those raw materials from the open marketplace, the company had been subjected to high and volatile prices, which put tremendous pressure on its profit margins.

The plan was for the joint venture company to be headquartered in the United States, employ more than five thousand people globally, and have revenues of approximately $11 billion.[33] It would manufacture such chemicals as polyethylene, polypropylene, and polycarbonate, which are chemicals used to make plastic for food packaging, beverage containers, and a variety of other products.

Both companies would have a 50 percent ownership, and because Dow was contributing the basic assets of the new organization, it would receive $9.5 billion from Kuwait. This deal was to be completed at the end of 2008, and joint operation was to begin on January 1, 2009.[34]

This Dow-Kuwait joint venture got right up to the point of being consummated when the folks in Kuwait suddenly announced they were backing away from the deal.[35] While this joint venture was being contemplated, the price of a barrel of oil had dropped from well over $100 down to the $40 range. Just how this caused Kuwait to look at the venture differently is not clear.[36] It's possible that the high-level government officials of Kuwait simply decided that they were nervous about the arrangement and decided to walk away. But Dow had put an enormous amount of effort into getting this joint venture together, only to have it collapse virtually days before the arrangement was to be finalized. One serious implication of this collapsed deal was that Dow had anticipated the infusion of the $9.5 billion, pretax, of cash in its funding strategy for an upcoming acquisition, so the company had to scramble to line up loans and other funding mechanisms.[37] The lesson here is clear: beware of potential partners who are vastly different from you and have no track record of joint efforts.

Let's take a look at another joint venture, which, unlike Dow, managed to get off the ground and even have some initial success. Unfortunately, like that of most joint ventures, its success was short lived.

In the late 1990s, Ericsson was really having major problems in the mobile phone business. Although it had good technology and strong relationships with the telecommunication operators, it was weak in manufacturing and the consumer aspects of product development. In 2000, one of Ericsson's major suppliers had a debilitating fire in its plant and caused Ericsson to miss out on the huge 47 percent growth in the mobile phone industry that year.[38] Then it was beset by quality-control problems in getting production up and running again.[39] Also, because Ericsson is primarily an engineering-dominated company, with inadequate marketing and consumer focus, it missed the demand for sleeker models of mobile phones with a variety of sophisticated new features. These setbacks caused Ericsson to lose significant market share and suffer financially.

At the same time, another mobile phone manufacturer, Sony, was also having big difficulties. Although it had good consumer electronics experience and manufacturing capabilities, it was really weak in two areas: (1) the core technologies of cell phones and (2) relationships with the telecommunication operators. To solve each other's problems, in 2001 Sony and Ericsson got together to form a joint venture. It appeared that the matchup was a good one. Ericsson brought the telecommunication operator relationships and good technology; Sony brought the manufacturing and the consumer aspect of the business. Although Sony Ericsson had some difficult times at first, by the third quarter of 2003, the joint venture made its first profit, $115 million on revenue of $2.2 billion.[40] The joint venture was a 50–50 relationship, so the profits were split evenly.

Although joint ventures have a reputation for being hard to manage, this one initially went fairly well. For example, in 2004 Sony Ericsson launched its new 5700 phone, one of the first to offer video streaming, a music capability, and a 1.3 megapixel camera.[41] It was also able to develop and market the first-ever cell phone built around the Microsoft Windows Mobile operating system.[42]

Unfortunately, by 2009, some of the typical problems related to joint ventures started to emerge with this Sony Ericsson arrangement. Most important, the innovation rate fell off, and as a result, the joint venture was being hurt by exciting new products from Nokia and Samsung. The venture's cutback in R&D, which, as I noted earlier, often occurs as each partner favors primarily supporting things it 100 percent owns, caused Sony Ericsson to be late in entering the smart-phone market. In fact, it was so far behind in product development that the joint venture would have needed to make a big investment just to catch up.[43] Further, the market itself was being hurt badly by the 2008–2009 financial crisis. Sony Ericsson announced in March 2009 that it projected a loss of

$528 million in the first quarter of 2009.[44] As stated in the *Wall Street Journal,* "Sony Ericsson only has itself to blame."[45]

For Sony, the negative result was really not much of a drag on its financial health, given the sheer size of its overall business. In contrast, the poor performance was a serious problem for Ericsson because the joint venture had been representing almost 25 percent of its operating profit in 2007.[46] As the *Wall Street Journal* noted, "Eight years on, it is still the source of Ericsson's problems rather than an answer to them. It is time to finish the process and quit the venture for good."[47] The Sony Ericsson joint venture may have seemed like a great idea initially, but over time some of the obvious risks became reality and caused significant problems.

◾◾◾

You know that I don't think joint ventures are a good idea. Sometimes they work, but more often than not they fail. If you are considering a joint venture or partnership, following these simple rules will help you yield significantly better results than Dow and Sony Ericsson did:

- *Avoid complicated arrangements.* If you are pursuing a joint venture, keep it simple. If the arrangements are too complicated, the probability is quite high that the effort will be very difficult to execute. Complicated arrangements also eat up a lot of management time and talent. To achieve the needed simplicity, secure mutual agreement up front as to how key decisions will be made, the percentage of revenue that will be allocated to R&D each year, and any other important operating guidelines.
- *Don't underestimate cultural clashes.* Do your homework about the culture of the organization with which you are considering partnering. Most negotiations focus on the financial aspects, the technology involved, manufacturing capabilities, and so on. More critical to success is gauging the basic cultures of the partnering organizations and whether or not there will eventually be a serious clash.

- *Consider dropping the idea.* Before you invest resources in finding a partner or forming a joint venture because you need to fill some obvious skill or capability gap in your organization, I urge you to give serious consideration to killing the whole idea. Although a project might look very attractive, be objective about whether you can really pull it off in a simple, reasonable way. Joint ventures and partnerships are seldom simple, and they seldom endure over time.

Joint ventures are seductive. On paper, they can look like a way for both parties to win, but more often, the reality is quite different. Let's face it: if you own only half of something, over time you're just not going to give it the tender loving care you give to something for which you are totally responsible. It's human nature.

# 11

## PRINCIPLE X

# Shake Up the Organization

E stablished organizations often have a very difficult time achieving dramatic innovation that will have a major impact on the performance of the company. This is because they have comfortably settled into a routine for managing the business, and it's natural to become convinced that you have figured things out and there is no need for change. Let's take a look at a few classic examples of this syndrome.

In 1994, Sony introduced a revolutionary video game console, the PlayStation. Over the next ten years, the Sony PlayStation really established the computer game business, primarily among teenagers. PlayStation II was an absolute rage. Given its success, Microsoft followed in 2001 with its own product, called Xbox. Sony then became focused on strengthening the capabilities of its PlayStation II and, in 2006, finally emerged with a new product called PlayStation III, which was, frankly, more of the same but faster and with some more features. The same was true for Microsoft. It developed the Xbox 360 which was, like PlayStation III, more of the same.

The real innovation in the computer game business was the emergence of the Nintendo Wii in 2006. The Wii was a completely new product with a completely new target audience. It truly appealed to the masses. Nintendo's Wii was a family game machine that could be used by young and old. It even had an extensive exercise regime. It sold as successfully to nursing homes as it did to the everyday household. By the end of 2008, Nintendo Wii had the dominant global market share in the computer game business.[1] Meanwhile, PlayStation III and Microsoft Xbox 360 were slugging it out for the remainder of the business while continuing to focus on male teenagers, the traditional computer game crowd.

Sony and Microsoft are powerful organizations with massive resources, but they were trapped in their own idea of what a computer game machine was supposed to be. Clearly those two organizations will need to shake things up in their game divisions if they are going to innovate new ideas that will give them the edge in the marketplace.

The bookstore giant Barnes and Noble is another organization that just didn't manage to shake things up and missed a huge opportunity. In the mid-1990s, when the Internet was emerging, it would have been logical for Barnes and Noble to jump on the Internet and develop an easy way for customers to buy books online. Instead, Amazon came from nowhere to develop that business and today absolutely owns the online ordering of books. Amazon did it again recently when it developed the Kindle, a handheld electronic book that allows readers to download, store, and conveniently read books without the bulkiness of the paper versions. Given the incredible depth of experience in the book business that Barnes and Noble represents, it really is interesting that it has not been capable of generating these fundamental innovations.

When you leave organizations alone but ask them to innovate, in all probability the ideas that emerge will be subtle variations on what they are already doing. If you want major innovation, you really have to shake up the organization. The rest of this chapter provides some helpful suggestions for doing so.

## INSERT FRESH TALENT

One mistake that organizations make over and over is leaving people in key jobs too long. Managers begin to believe that it would be a big risk to the organization to move these experienced people. What they seldom realize until it's too late is that by leaving the "experienced" person in place, they are passing up a big opportunity to bring in a bunch of bright new ideas on how to run things and excite customers. You need to regularly insert fresh talent into your organization at all levels to create and inspire new ideas and to stay on the edge of innovation.

In July 2007, IBM shook things up by naming John E. Kelly to be the head of its corporate research laboratories. Those laboratories were established in 1945 and are generally regarded as among the world's best corporate research labs.[2] However, at the time Kelly took over, multiple projects were being pursued, at the risk of spreading the overall investment too thin.[3] The main risk of spreading the investment over many projects is that the big ideas, which in the information technology business require very large budgets, get underfunded. Thus, they take too long, risking competitive preemption. Another issue Kelly was addressing was the fact that IBM was risking losing its leadership role if it didn't generate a breakthrough in the evolution of the semiconductor and in tapping the power of clusters of computers. With all this in mind, and after only six months in the role, Kelly launched some major changes intended to increase the overall impact of the labs. Most important, he reorganized the labs to pursue four critically important research priorities.

The four projects Kelly selected were quite large; each would require over $100 million in investments over two to three years, and each had the goal of generating revenue of at least $1 billion per year.[4] The projects were to (1) develop a successor to the current semiconductor; (2) design computers that process data more efficiently; (3) apply mathematics to solve complex business problems; and (4) assemble massive clusters of computers that operate like a single machine—often referred to as "cloud" computing.[5] Each of these represented enormous technical challenges and enormous potential payoffs. This degree of focus represented a major change for IBM.

Kelly also developed plans to create numerous joint projects with other science laboratories operated by countries, companies, and independent research organizations in an attempt to globalize research and revitalize R&D. Kelly believed that "the nature of research itself is changing. Great ideas are springing up everywhere, and we need to shift from focusing on large bricks-and-mortar operations to having a much more collaborative outreach program."[6] An example of one such collaboration was an initiative with Saudi Arabia that was focused on nanotechnology.

The fact that Kelly's collaborative research strategy emerged from his prior assignment at IBM as the head of its chip business demonstrates the benefit of moving people around within an organization. As head of the chip business, Kelly saw huge financial losses for IBM as it tried to keep up with the latest technology. This caused him to do an unusual thing: he set up a number of research alliances with several partners, including Sony Electronics and Advanced Micro Devices, in order to share expenses and collaborate technically.[7] This fresh approach enabled IBM's chip business to return to profitability while also having an easier time staying on the cutting edge of technology. Kelly took this experience with him to the research laboratories, where he was able to successfully partner with various countries and organizations to rejuvenate IBM's research capabilities.

In 2003, Merck Pharmaceuticals also wanted to stimulate its R&D. There's probably no organization within Merck quite as important as the large R&D operation, which is responsible for producing new drugs, Merck's core source of revenue. Back in 2003, Merck, like the rest of the large pharmaceutical companies, found it more and more difficult to develop new drugs, and it needed to name a new head of research to generate some fresh ideas. They reached for an individual named Peter Kim, who had joined Merck in 2001 in research, but prior to 2001 had spent most of his career as a biologist at MIT. Putting someone with virtually no Merck experience in such a key job was quite a testimony to the value Merck placed on getting some fresh thinking in the organization. As *Fortune* said, "As an outsider in a place with a clubby, insider culture, Kim had a perspective long time employees lacked,"[8] and Merck was very much in need of new perspective.

Similar to John E. Kelly of IBM, Kim brought a belief that the research efforts at Merck needed to be far more collaborative with organizations outside Merck. He also launched a major effort to make sure that Merck scientists were adequately mining the scientific literature to identify promising compounds that could potentially emerge as blockbuster drugs. He encouraged scientists not only to work with organizations outside Merck to identify new compounds but also to seriously consider acquisition of those efforts if it looked as though the technology was promising and had long-term potential.

Kim's efforts have had a real impact. In the year prior to Kim's being put in charge of Merck's research laboratories, Merck had entered into just ten licensing deals. During Kim's third full year in the job, after his collaboration mind-set was implemented, Merck executed fifty-three joint licensing deals and acquisitions.[9]

▨ ▨ ▨

Both of these examples show that—be it reaching for someone on the outside, as Merck did with Peter Kim, or taking a strong-performing individual from another part of the company, as IBM did with John E. Kelly—putting fresh talent into key jobs yields real benefits.

Here are some lessons I've learned that can be valuable reminders as you think through your staffing, particularly staffing related to key jobs:

- *Don't let people get set in their ways.* It's natural to be proud of the way you do things and the results you achieve. Within organizations people will protect existing practices more strongly with every passing month and push back against any kind of change. You can't let this happen. If part of your organization is stagnant, you need to insert some fresh talent to stimulate new ideas and new ways of doing things.
- *Don't always make the obvious choice.* I'm confident that most folks at IBM and Merck thought that when the replacement for the corporate R&D organization was named, it would be a person with long tenure at the company who had spent most of his career in corporate R&D. To get really fresh thinking and high energy, you need to look very broadly. Consequently, often the choice won't be

the obvious candidate. That's good. It says clearly that the goal is change and improved results.

* *Evolve.* The world is constantly changing. This is true in virtually all aspects of life, including the technologies that underpin your products and processes. But as employees get settled into a rhythm of doing work, they become less and less likely to jump out in front of new trends and capitalize on them. Your organization needs to evolve with the times, and sometimes the only way to do that is to shake things up by bringing new talent and new ideas into the business. Your survival could depend on it.

Too often leaders think it is necessary to keep people in place for long periods of time because their experience is valuable. And often, when there is a change in leadership, people believe it's necessary to select someone from within the organization who knows the ropes. But doing this has huge risks. "Experienced" people tend to cling to the prior practices of the organization, and nothing changes. Inserting fresh talent is the best way to bring about change.

## REORGANIZE TO WIN

It takes a lot of courage for a leader to seize a great idea and quickly reorganize around that idea to implement it. This is true of a new product, significant upgrades to a current product, or a major internal process improvement. There is a lot of momentum in an organization, and breaking that momentum to point the troops in a new direction is hard. Though such a change will often generate fear, it also gets the innovative juices flowing and will motivate employees who have the self-confidence and capabilities to step up, tackle the future, and produce significant results.

Canon is a company that embraces change and has consistently demonstrated the ability to reorganize to win. Fujio Mitarai started with Canon in 1966 as an accountant. He made very rapid progress and ran Canon USA for most of the 1980s. He was named CEO of Canon in 1995 and has done a spectacular job since then, turning Canon into an incredibly successful company. During his tenure, Canon has become the world's largest manufacturer of office copying equipment and moved ahead of Sony to become the world's largest maker of digital cameras.[10]

Traditionally, Canon has been a company run primarily by engineers. The company has done a terrific job over the years of attracting Japanese technical talent and entrepreneurs and has invested heavily in R&D. Unfortunately, in the 1980s, things became rather chaotic, particularly in the Canon product divisions headquartered in Japan. As aptly noted by *Fortune,* "Canon was developing into a clutch of warring fiefdoms, each with its own strategy and free to lavish capital and manpower on pet projects without regard for the rest of the company. Money losing ventures plodded along year after year, siphoning resources from products with genuine promise. The company's debt ballooned."[11] Concerning this period, Mitarai commented that the company seemed to suffer "a collapse of its central nervous system."[12]

In 1989, Mitarai moved out of his job running Canon USA to assume an executive role at Canon's Japanese headquarters. The years following this appointment were quite frustrating. He commented, "I offered all kinds of suggestions for reform, but no one listened. They were all techies. It was as if I spoke a different language."[13]

These years of frustration equipped Mitarai to tackle with real gusto the CEO job, which he was given in 1995. He quickly shut down Canon's personal computer business because it was losing money and, in the ensuing four years, he closed down an additional six money-losing divisions, such as liquid crystal displays, photovoltaic batteries, and electric typewriters. These moves shocked the business community in Japan, but Mitarai's strategy was clear. He wanted to ride the winners and constantly improve them, and put the struggling divisions out of their pain.

When Mitarai took over the CEO job, he was saddled with a debt of $7.5 billion.[14] He knew cost cutting had to be right at the top of his agenda, while also making sure that the promising divisions really delivered for the company. The profitable products that Mitarai decided to focus on were copiers, printers, and cameras.

In his effort to clean up the company, Mitarai retained a great regard for R&D. He continued to grow that part of the company, and by 2004, Canon's R&D budget was $2.5 billion. He publicly stated at that time that he wanted to grow this budget to $4.5 billion.[15] He also put a high priority on filing patents, and by the end of 2005, Canon ranked second to IBM as the recipient of the most new U.S. patents.

Mitarai's finance background really showed through in the intensity with which he tackled cost management. He reorganized groups around new systems and processes in order to lower cost and increase effectiveness. One such process that Mitarai championed was a new manufacturing process that he called cell-production. It reorganized the traditional assembly line into small teams of workers who produced entire products in carefully orchestrated sequential steps. Cell-production was a resounding success. It generated significant gains in productivity and dealt with the age-old problem of production lines: speed being dictated by the slowest worker. By the year 2000, more than twelve miles of conveyor belts were replaced with cell-production stations, resulting in significant cuts in inventory, faster response time by manufacturing, and the ability to bring new designs online much quicker.[16]

Mitarai also led cost-trimming efforts in other parts of the company. For example, in 2006 an effort was launched to reorganize and overhaul the procurement process; it reduced procurement costs by $1.1 billion.[17] He also led the charge to find yet another new manufacturing approach that would be even more efficient than the revolutionary cell-production practice. His idea was to triple the number of robots used at Canon by 2008.[18] At the lead plant that makes Canon toner cartridges, this approach reduced the number of assembly workers by 85 percent.[19]

Mitarai is constantly organizing to win by cutting what is unproductive and reorganizing the company to focus on high-potential divisions. He is also constantly reviewing the processes used in the functional areas of the company, such as manufacturing, and pushing for more and more innovation and larger savings so that Canon can quickly get out in front and stay there.

Mitarai's constant efforts to shake up the organization have paid off handsomely for Canon. After ten years as the CEO, Mitarai drove Canon's operating margins to over 15 percent, which put them at three times the level of other leading consumer electronics firms.[20] The market capitalization of Canon has increased by more than a factor of three during Mitarai's reign.[21]

＊＊＊

Mitarai teaches us a very valuable lesson: reorganize around the important things and put aside those that are clearly not working. He also shows us that being this successful with reorganization takes a lot of strength and a certain amount of ruthlessness. You need to try bold new things, but also to shut down the things that don't work.

Here are a few tips you need to keep in mind as you strive to organize to achieve innovation excellence:

- *Hold out for the really strong ideas.* Reorganizing your company around solid but average ideas wastes time and resources. You need to be very selective in deciding what ideas to jump on to generate big improvement. So often, managers make compromises or lower standards so that the new approaches pursued have only a modest impact at best. The courageous leader sets very high standards in deciding to pursue an initiative.
- *Set priorities.* Don't confuse the organization by trying to do too many things at once. Pick one or two very big ideas, and put all other innovation projects aside. There is nothing like tight focus on a key effort to make it clear what the organization is trying to do.
- *Form a new organization and hold it responsible.* You want to assemble a group of people who have as their sole responsibility the successful implementation of the innovative idea. The head of the new group

needs to have a significant track record of success and must report high enough in the organization that he can get the help he needs to get things done in a timely manner and with excellence. Other members of the group should also be strong performers. It should be noted that to be placed into a group like this, with a very important and well-defined goal, is invigorating.

- *Minimize the involvement of the current organization.* The current organization is busy carrying out today's work. No doubt you may have to tap into things they do or into experience they have, but that should be done with the full realization that their first priority, and what they are comfortable with, is carrying out their current responsibilities. Also, they have a built-in bias for how things are currently being done, so if you rely on them too heavily, you really aren't giving a fair chance to the new group and the new approach.

Reorganizing is a powerful tool for a leader. Relying on the current organization typically won't work in achieving significant change. When people are left in their current roles but asked to do new things, their first priority will be doing what they've been doing in the past. Consequently, you really aren't giving your new approaches a fair chance. There is no better way to make it clear to the organization that innovation and change are high priorities than to seize a clever, high-potential idea and form a new group of highly talented people whose only responsibility is to make that idea a big success.

## CREATE INTENSE MARKETPLACE FOCUS

Organizations regularly make two huge mistakes regarding the marketplace. First, they get into too many businesses and end up diluting their efforts and performing poorly everywhere. We saw this earlier with Canon. After Mitarai became CEO, he discontinued seven different business divisions so that Canon could focus on copiers, printers, and cameras. Second, companies become lazy, particularly after experiencing some stability or success, and they pay inadequate attention to their customers and to their distribution channels. They allow their products to fall out of favor, and they miss inflection points. A strong leader creates intense focus on the marketplace and does not get into that position.

Focus was something Philips, the Dutch electronics company, had major problems with in the late 1990s and early 2000s. Though over a hundred years old, Philips found itself in a real mess. It was in too many businesses, and it was extremely sloppy about how it was executing in the marketplace.

One of its challenges concerned a $250 million advertising campaign in the United States to promote its new flat-screen TVs. Although the ads were quite attention catching, Philips had big production problems, and the advertising ran for six months without any product in the distribution channel.[22] That example pretty much sums up the challenges that Philips was having during this period.

Philips typically produced very good products from a technical perspective, but it consistently faltered in executing the marketing and sales plans to support its products. For example, Philips was quite innovative during the very early days of the cell phone, and as noted by Gerald Kleisterlee, who became the CEO of Philips in 2001, "Philips could have been a top three player in cell phones if we had done things right from a marketing point of view."[23] The fact is that Nokia, Ericsson, and Motorola out-executed Philips, and after Philips struggled in the cell phone business for years, the only role left for the company was to supply components to these major players in that industry.

Philips's pattern of missing commercial opportunities, even though it had industry-leading technology in its grasp, continued throughout the 1990s. After just over a year in the CEO job, Kleisterlee grew very frustrated with this lack of marketplace focus and with the Philips management that allowed this to happen. Kleisterlee made this clear when he indicated that Philips's top management was simply "too old, too male, and too Dutch."[24] Most of the top management of Philips had spent their career with the company, came from the technical side of the business, and spent most of their time with Philips in Eindhoven, the small, southern Dutch city where the company was founded in 1891.

The focus on the technical side of the business over the decades caused Philips to typically be insensitive to key sales issues. This really hurt them in the consumer electronics industry, which is dependent on effective retail execution in order to be successful. Larry Blanford, who was hired in 2001 to figure out how to make Philips Consumer Electronics successful, commented that Philips was "absolutely the worst supplier to our customers in the U.S. consumer electronics industry."[25] Philips was notoriously ineffective in important retail stores due to its lack of relationships with key retail personnel.[26] This kind of behavior led to huge business problems for Philips: although one-third of its revenue was related to consumer electronics offerings by the company, that part of the business had an operating margin of only 2.4 percent. By comparison, the appliance business operating margin was 17.5 percent and lighting was 12.5 percent.[27]

Demonstrating the lack of priority on sales execution in its U.S. consumer electronics business, Philips had only fifteen people on its national sales team to call on large U.S. retailers, whereas its main competitors had hundreds.[28] An additional problem was that management couldn't decide what the sales priorities should be. At times, managers placed very severe short-term sales targets on the division, which caused the existing salespeople, few as there were, to try to apply high pressure to the retailers to load up with the faster-moving, lower-margin Philips products. To do this, sales focused on the very large retailers like Target and Walmart, where they would be able to move a lot of volume quickly. Then, a few months later, management would decide profit was more important, causing the salespeople to redirect their efforts to specialty retailers where slower-moving but higher-margin products did well and to ignore the large retailers. This kind of behavior clearly demonstrates that the management of the company had no conceptual feel for the retail marketplace and its importance in consumer electronics.

All this lack of focus on marketplace execution and overemphasis on technology was hurting the company financially. In 2001, Philips lost

$976 million; sales fell almost 20 percent.[29] During 2002, the stock price of Philips dropped roughly 50 percent and by March 2003 was down to $15 per share from $45 in mid-2000. Although some of these financial challenges were caused by impairment charges and write-downs on outside investments, the stock price drop showed that the marketplace was beginning to run out of patience.

CEO Kleisterlee had his hands full. The core issue that he had to tackle was the fact that Philips had no focus. It was rightfully viewed as a conglomerate, participating in a very wide range of businesses, such as light bulbs, electric shavers, defibulators, and MRI machines.[30] Believe it or not, it was even in the music business; it had such artists as Sting and Elton John under contract, and their music was produced by the Philips PolyGram label. This created great confusion in the financial markets, as you couldn't benchmark Philips against any one industry.

To tackle this problem of lack of focus, one of the early steps taken by Kleisterlee was to sell off the semiconductor business. It had been notoriously volatile, and sales of Philips semiconductors dropped 30 percent in the 2001–2002 period.[31] As it swung from profit to loss, it caused great volatility in the Philips stock price, even though it was consistently earning good margins in some of its other areas, such as medical devices. One of the VPs at Philips commented, "What good is it being in lighting and medical if your stock moves with the SOX semiconductor index?"[32]

After selling off semiconductors, Kleisterlee reorganized the company into four easy-to-understand units: medical, lighting, consumer electronics, and domestic appliances. Making Philips lean and market focused really caught the attention of the financial community. In the years prior to Kleisterlee, the company's credibility was extremely low; it was viewed as unfocused and committed to the status quo. By focusing on four specific areas, Kleisterlee changed all that and made it clear to the financial world that he was turning things around.[33]

Another step that Kleisterlee took was to move the manufacturing of Philips low-end products from Europe to Asia, where labor was significantly cheaper. For a hundred-plus-year-old European company to move manufacturing out of the region to Asia took enormous nerve. But it sent a great signal to the organization that it was a new ball game for Philips.

Kleisterlee knew he needed different kinds of personnel to lead this company for it to be truly market focused. The company's headquarters and R&D center of Eindhoven was a real problem from a recruiting standpoint. As observed by *Fortune,* "While Eindhoven's tranquil ambience may make it an ideal place for conceptual breakthroughs about the next generation of electric fan heaters, it isn't the sort of environment that breeds market-savvy executives with a global outlook."[34] To achieve that market focus, the head office of Philips was moved to Amsterdam. This gave the company better access to strong talent, who typically want to live in a vibrant place. It also put it closer to the financial community, giving the financial analysts easier access to company executives and hence making the company easier to follow.

Philips sold off and shut down numerous business units that no longer fit into the four areas of market focus that Kleisterlee selected. Also, facilities serving the remaining four divisions were greatly consolidated. By 2007, Phillips was down to seventy factories that produced lighting (from 110 in the late 1990s), and the majority of those seventy were in low-wage countries.[35] Kleisterlee did a great job of moving low-end manufacturing to outsource vendors and only retaining the more challenging manufacturing tasks in-house.

Kleisterlee also had Philips establish numerous joint ventures, even with such competitors as Korea's LG. For example, Philips owns 33 percent of LG Philips LCD, a joint venture with LG that has a market value of over $3 billion. The company also acquired 100 percent of a small lighting technology called Lumileds from Agilent Technology in Silicon Valley and spent almost $2 billion acquiring health care companies such as Intermagnetics, a manufacturer of components for MRI machines.[36]

By 2007, all these moves by Kleisterlee were having a significant marketplace impact. In the first six months of that calendar year, Philips stock returned to the $45 level, triple the low point in 2003 and a number last seen in the year 2000.

There are powerful lessons here regarding the importance of creating intense focus on the marketplace. A strong leader needs to make sure everyone in the organization understands that focusing on a small number of product areas where you can clearly win and making that win happen via laser-like market focus are key.

Here are some courageous practices that you need to put into place to create the same kind of marketplace focus in your organization:

- *Do business in a small number of industries where you can win.* When large companies expand into various different industries, they often end up struggling in their core businesses. We saw in the beginning of this book how Fiat fell into this trap by losing focus on cars and becoming involved in too many different businesses, such as insurance, publishing, energy, farm equipment, and several other industries. Although there are some exceptions, in most cases organizations function best when they've carefully selected a few specific markets they are convinced they can conquer and focus their attention on excelling in those industries. Take a look at your organization and objectively assess how many totally different and independent efforts are being pursued. You'll need real courage to set priorities and shut down efforts that have been going for years. But a strong leader faces up to these things and makes these decisions.

- *Move in the merchants.* You need to select people for key positions who have a real sense of the marketplace and enjoy creating excellence with regard to products, distribution channels, and consumer experiences.

- *Focus on product, channel, and consumer excellence.* Are your products better than those of the competition or not? If not, how many months is it going to take to achieve that position? Who is the leader of the effort to make that happen? Talk to the people in the distribution channel regularly and see how they view the individuals in your organization with whom they interact, and their practices. Set up a regular quantitative survey of the distribution channel to see how your strengths and weaknesses compare to the competition. Is someone in charge of carefully watching consumer behavior and figuring out the unarticulated needs your products could be modified to satisfy? Too often, managers are sloppy and don't nail these product, channel, and consumer issues, even though doing so can make the difference between success and failure. A strong leader needs to provide intense focus on them.

- *Create a sense of marketplace urgency.* You need to remind your organization regularly that success in the marketplace is your most important measure. All of your people need to understand the urgency in fixing problems, coming up with consumer and retail innovations, and getting out in front. Openly discussing your market shares, the performance of your products versus those of the competition, customer surveys, and the feedback from distribution channel visits really helps establish the importance of these matters. Your very public focus on achieving marketplace success is essential.

Reorganizing, putting strong performers in key jobs, and keeping the focus on customers are powerful tools you should be using to shake up your organization so that it can implement new, high-potential, innovative ideas. By doing this, you will be on your way to establishing a strong business driven by strong leadership.

# Conclusion

You—yes, you—can be that leader who has the courage to face the tough decisions and achieve operational and innovative excellence. The principles I outlined in this book will, I hope, inspire you to step up and take charge. Let's briefly revisit the ten principles and be very clear about the kinds of actions you can take to lead your organization, be it small, medium, or large, to make big progress.

**Principle I: Devise a Demanding Game Plan to Confront Reality.** You need to isolate one or two things that will dramatically improve the impact of your organization, and develop the vision for what needs to be done, the strategies for achieving it, and the measures that show whether the vision is being achieved.

**Principle II: Staff for Success.** You need an ongoing, high-quality performance appraisal system to spot the superstars and develop them, and to confront the weak performers to either quickly improve or move out. Employee surveys can help determine which managers are strong leaders and which are struggling. These steps ensure that you will have the talent to properly staff and execute your game plan for success.

**Principle III: Clean Up the Sloppiness.** The basic processes and systems used to run the organization should be the minimum required, free of bells and whistles and excessive exceptions. Each system should be the responsibility of a specific person who is evaluated by specific measures of efficiency and effectiveness for his or her process or system. Bureaucracy should be minimized through accountability, minimal layers, and maximum spans.

**Principle IV: Institutionalize Tight-Fisted Cost Control.** This is not hard; it just takes nerve. Put the clamps on any budget under your control. Then start looking for marginally useful projects and activities that you can close down or significantly pare back or outsource to a less expensive but equally effective vendor in another part of the world, enabling you to cut your budget further. You need to realize that the human instinct is to hire more people, thinking you are becoming more important to the organization. Just the opposite is true. The emerging talent that gets noticed are those that manage budgets tightly and innovate while doing so.

**Principle V: Insist on Functional Excellence.** When it comes to tapping functional resources, strong leaders know to reach for talented, highly principled individuals who know not only their area of expertise but also when and how to apply it. They won't just be order takers; they will push back. Also, they understand when things should be done one way as a company and when to allow exceptions. They will also fight off the tendency to do too many things; instead they will focus on the few efforts that are of high impact.

**Principle VI: Create a Culture of Innovation.** You as the leader of your organization need to create the mind-set that everyone in the organization is constantly looking for bright ideas that will generate significant improvement. The emotional rewards in your organization need to reflect this mind-set. Really big ideas are staffed and pursued with gusto; the other ideas are put aside. Also, even as you encourage continual improvement for processes, you protect your innovators so that they feel free to risk failure while pursuing the big-impact ideas.

**Principle VII: Demand Accountability and Decisiveness; Avoid Consensus.** When an individual is involved in a decision that requires the agreement of several people, the responsibility for the result is spread out, which tends to cause those participating to primarily protect their interests rather than do what is best for the total effort. Also, the participants tend not to be as thorough in their probing for the best option, because a bad result can be blamed on others. A courageous leader makes sure that each specific effort has a specific individual accountable for the result.

**Principle VIII: Exploit Inflection Points.** You need to be constantly on the lookout for a new technology or emerging customer trend that has the potential to generate significant improvement in what you are doing. Seeking out and exploiting inflection points needs to be a key value and priority in your organization. Strong leaders know to select experienced, customer-focused individuals for key positions and charge them to be on the lookout for those key inflection points.

**Principle IX: Value Ideas from Anywhere.** As a leader, you need to make it clear to your people that you want ideas from any- where and anyone regarding ways to generate significant improvement. Although you may charge a particular person or group with refining and implementing the ideas, everyone should be on the lookout. Beware of a situation where the ownership of an idea or effort is shared with another organization not under your control. Such partnerships or joint efforts are very risky, as typically they lead to neither party's being fully committed.

**Principle X: Shake Up the Organization.** If you leave the people and the organization structure alone, you will yield about the same results tomorrow as you do today. To successfully implement a new idea or change, you need fresh talent, and you need to reorganize around the new effort. That way, you issue a clear signal that things will be different and that you highly value the new effort. To ensure success, you need to staff the effort with top performers who possess a strong customer focus.

▨▨▨

Implementing these principles requires courage, but these principles and the reasoning behind them are easy to explain to your people. Taking action will earn you their respect and will generate the excitement that is required to get an organization going in a positive direction.

Now go out there and be bold. Be very clear that you have a decisive plan, that you are not afraid to take action, to do what's right even when it's hard. It's difficult for any leader to put himself or herself on the line, to take a public risk, but that is exactly what you must do. No one needs a leader for inaction, to preserve the status quo.

Your newfound energy and resolve will inspire your team, and even should they not agree with you, they will respect you. With these ten principles to guide you, with this road map of the difficult situations that require your decisiveness, nothing will hold you—or your organization—back!

# NOTES

## Introduction

1. Charles Burck, "Will Success Spoil General Motors?" *Fortune*, August 22, 1983, *108*(4), 94–101.

2. Ibid.

3. David Welch, "What Could Dull Toyota's Edge?" *Business Week Online*, April 17, 2008.

4. Stuart Gannes,"GM Is Tougher Than You Think," *Fortune*, November 10, 1986, *114*(9), 57.

5. "Top Picks: Best Models of the Year," *Consumer Reports*, April 2009, *74*(4), 6.

6. Ibid.

## Chapter 1

1. Stephan Faris, "The Turn Around," *Fortune International*, May 14, 2007, *155*(8), 32.

2. Janet Guyan, "Running on Empty," *Fortune*, December 30, 2002, *146*(13), 125.

3. Gail Edmondson, "Running on Empty: Management Is in Turmoil," *Business Week*, May 13, 2002, no. 3782, pp. 26–33.

4. Faris, "The Turn Around," pp. 32–40.

5. Ibid.

6. Edmonson, "Running on Empty: Management Is in Turmoil," p. 27.

7. Guyan, "Running on Empty," pp. 125–132.

8. Ibid.

9. Edmondson, "Running on Empty: Management Is in Turmoil," p. 29.

10. Faris, "The Turn Around," p. 33.

11. Faris, "The Turn Around."

12. Ibid.

13. Faris, "The Turn Around," p. 39.

14. Amarendra Bhushan, "Fiat (Fix It Again, Tony)—Chrysler Merger: What Do They Get Out of It?" *CEOWORLD Magazine Online,* June 16, 2009.

15. Ibid.

16. Faris, "The Turn Around."

17. Edmonson, "Running on Empty: Management Is in Turmoil."

18. Gail Edmondson and David Welch, "Fiat Is in Deep, Deep Trouble," *Business Week,* December 13, 2004, no. 3912, pp. 56–58.

19. Ibid.

20. Edmondson, "Running on Empty: Management Is in Turmoil."

21. "Fiat's Turnaround Takes Root," *Business Week Online,* November 13, 2006.

22. Eric Sylvers, "Fiat Chairman Leaving to Make Room for Agnelli," *New York Times Online,* February 26, 2003.

23. Edmondson, "Running on Empty: Management Is in Turmoil."

24. Faris, "The Turn Around," p. 35.

25. Edmondson and Welch, "Fiat Is in Deep, Deep Trouble."

26. Faris, "The Turn Around," p. 33.

27. Ibid.

28. Faris, "The Turn Around."

29. Ibid.

30. Ibid., p. 35.

31. Faris, "The Turn Around."

32. David Rocks, "Fiat to Return to the U.S.," *Business Week Online,* June 9, 2008.

33. "Fiat's Turnaround Takes Root."

34. Paul Betts, "Fiat Shows Rival Carmakers the Tough Route to Survival," *Financial Times,* March 31, 2009, p. 16.

35. "Fiat's Turnaround Takes Root."

36. Faris, "The Turn Around."

37. Rocks, "Fiat to Return to the U.S."

38. Betts, "Fiat Shows Rival Carmakers."

39. Ibid.

## Chapter 2

1. Jack Welch, *Winning* (New York: HarperCollins, 2005).

2. Carol Loomis, "The Tragedy of General Motors," *Fortune,* February 20, 2006, *153*(3), 60–71.

3. "Vodafone's Tough Calls," *Business Week Online,* February 28, 2006.

4. Ibid.

5. Ibid.

6. Kerry Capell, "How to Fix Vodafone," *Business Week Online,* June 7, 2006.

7. Ibid.

8. Ibid.

9. Steve Rosenbush, "Vodafone Regains Its Balance," *Business Week Online,* October 20, 2006.

10. Joann Muller and Robyn Meredith, "Last Laugh," *Forbes,* April 18, 2005, *175*(8), 98–101.

11. Ibid.

12. Ibid.

13. Ibid., p. 100.

14. Jerry Flint, "Hyundai's Impatience," *Forbes Global,* June 4, 2007, *3*(3), 43–44.

15. Muller and Meredith, "Last Laugh."

16. Flint, "Hyundai's Impatience."

17. Katrina Brooker, "Jim Kilts Is an Old School Curmudgeon. Nothing Could Be Better for Gillette," *Fortune,* December 30, 2002, *146*(13), 94–103.

18. "A Fresh Face Could Do Wonders for Gillette," *Business Week*, November 6, 2000, no. 3706, pp. 52–53.

19. Brooker, "Jim Kilts," p. 95.

20. Ibid., p. 99.

21. Brooker, "Jim Kilts."

22. Spencer E. Ante, "Sprint's Wake-Up Call," *Business Week*, March 3, 2008, no. 4073, pp. 54–58.

23. Ibid., p. 55.

24. Ante, "Sprint's Wake-Up Call."

25. Ibid.

26. Ibid.

27. Ibid., p. 56.

28. Ibid., p. 57.

29. Ibid.

30. Ante, "Sprint's Wake-Up Call."

**Chapter 3**

1. Stratford Sherman, "Digital's Daring Comeback Plan," *Fortune*, January 14, 1991, *123*(1), 100–103.

2. Ibid., p. 103.

3. Gary McWilliams, "Crunch Time at DEC," *Business Week*, May 4, 1992, no. 3264, pp. 30–33.

4. Richard Rapaport, "Culture War: Route 128," *Forbes*, September 13, 1993, *152*(60), S54–S60.

5. Sherman, "Digital's Daring Comeback Plan."

**Chapter 4**

1. Justin Scheck, "Taming Technology Sprawl," *Wall Street Journal*, January 29, 2008, p. B3.

2. Peter Burrows, "Stopping the Sprawl at HP," *Business Week*, May 29, 2006, no. 3986, pp. 54–57.

3. Ibid.

4. Ibid.

5. Ibid., p. 55.

6. Ibid.

7. Burrows, "Stopping the Sprawl at HP."

8. Ibid.

9. Ibid.

10. Carol Matlack, "Is the Worst Over at Alcatel-Lucent?" *Business Week Online*, November 29, 2007.

11. Peggy Hollinger, Andrew Parker, and Paul Taylor, "Pressure Rises for Alcatel Overhaul," *Financial Times*, October 5, 2007, p. 16.

12. Peggy Hollinger and Paul Taylor, "Alcatel Outlook Uncertain as It Reports Biggest Loss Since Tie-Up," *Financial Times*, February 9, 2008, p. 19.

13. Hollinger, Parker, and Taylor, "Pressure Rises," p. 16.

14. Ibid.

15. Ibid.

16. Ibid.

17. Hollinger and Taylor, "Alcatel Outlook Uncertain."

18. Hollinger, Parker, and Taylor, "Pressure Rises," p. 16.

19. Matlack, "Is the Worst Over at Alcatel-Lucent?"

20. Hollinger, Parker, and Taylor, "Pressure Rises," p. 16.

21. Ellen Florian Kratz, "Avon Looks Ripe for a Rebound," *Fortune*, March 20, 2006, *153*(5), 170.

22. Nanette Byrnes, "Avon: More Cosmetic Changes," *Business Week*, March 12, 2007, no. 4025, pp. 62–64.

23. Kratz, "Avon Looks Ripe for a Rebound."

24. Ibid.

25. Byrnes, "Avon: More Cosmetic Changes."

**Chapter 5**

1. Richard Tomlinson, "Can Nestlé Be the Very Best?" *Fortune*, November 13, 2000, *142*(11), 353–359.

2. Carol Matlack, "Nestlé Is Starting to Slim Down at Last," *Business Week*, October 27, 2003, no. 3855, pp. 56–58.

3. Ibid., p. 56.

4. Ibid.

5. "Daring, Defying, to Grow—Nestlé," *Economist*, August 7, 2004, *372* (8387), 57.

6. Ibid.

7. Janet Guyon,"Getting the Bugs Out at Volkswagen," *Fortune*, October 13, 2003, *148*(8), 145–149.

8. Alex Taylor III, "Can America Fall in Love with VW Again?" *Fortune*, May 16, 2005, *151*(10), 129–132.

9. Guyon, "Getting the Bugs Out at Volkswagen."

10. Allison Fass, "The $75,000 People's Car," *Forbes*, October 27, 2003, *179*(9), 222–223.

11. Ibid.

12. Taylor, "Can America Fall in Love with VW Again?"

13. Guyon, "Getting the Bugs Out at Volkswagen," p. 148.

14. Taylor, "Can America Fall in Love with VW Again?" p. 130.

15. Taylor, "Can America Fall in Love with VW Again?"

16. Steve Hamm and Joshua Schneyer, "International Isn't Just IBM's First Name," *Business Week*, January 28, 2008, no. 4068, pp. 36 – 39.

17. Ibid.

18. Ibid.

19. Ibid.

20. Ibid.

21. Ibid.

22. Ibid.

23. Ibid.

24. Ibid.

25. Ibid.

**Chapter 6**

1. Nelson D. Schwartz, "Can BP Bounce Back?" *Fortune*, October 16, 2006, 154(8), 91.

2. Ibid., p. 93.

3. Schwartz, "Can BP Bounce Back?" pp. 90–95.

4. Ibid., p. 93.

5. Schwartz, "Can BP Bounce Back?"

6. Ibid.

7. Ibid.

8. Sheila McNulty, "BP Memo Attacks Its Leadership Strategy," *Financial Times*, December 18, 2006, p. 1.

9. Neil King, "BP Crew Focused on Costs: Congress," *Wall Street Journal*, June 15, 2010, p. A1.

10. Ibid.

11. Ibid.

12. Kate Linebaugh, "Honda's Flexible Plants Provide Edge," *Wall Street Journal*, September 23, 2008, p. B1.

13. Ibid.

14. Ibid.

15. Ibid.

16. "Honda's Independent Streak," *Business Week*, October 2, 2000, no. 3701, p. 152.

17. Linebaugh, "Honda's Flexible Plants Provide Edge."

18. Ibid.

19. Stuart F. Brown, "Growing Drugs Is a Tricky Business," *Fortune*, November 25, 2002, *146*(11), 176–181.

20. Ibid.

21. Ibid.

22. Ibid.

23. Ibid.

24. Ibid.

25. Ibid.

26. Ibid.

27. Ibid.

## Chapter 7

1. "Procter & Gamble: World's Foremost Hair Care Company," *Drug and Cosmetic Industry*, August 1996, *159*(2), 46.

2. "Steering Deere Clear of 'Commodity Hell,'" *Business Week Online*, November 22, 2006.

3. Ibid.

4. Ibid.

5. Ibid.

6. Ibid.

7. Ibid.

8. Michael Arndt, "Deere's Revolution on Wheels," *Business Week*, July 2, 2007, no. 4041, p. 78.

9. Ibid.

10. Ibid.

11. "Steering Deere Clear of 'Commodity Hell.'"

12. "At 3M, a Struggle Between Efficiency and Creativity," *Business Week*, June 11, 2007, no. 4038, p. 9.

13. "At 3M," pp. 8–11.

14. Ibid., p. 10.

15. Ibid., p. 10.

16. "At 3M."

17. Ibid.

18. Ibid.

19. Ibid., p. 8.

20. "At 3M."

21. Ibid.

22. Ibid., p. 10.

23. Michael Arndt, "3M's Seven Pillars of Innovation," *Business Week Online*, May 10, 2006.

24. Ibid.

25. "How Whirlpool Defines Innovation," *Business Week Online*, March 6, 2006.

## Chapter 8

1. David Kiley, "Ford's Most Important New Model," *Business Week Online*, January 9, 2007.

2. Ibid.

3. Ibid.

4. Ibid.

5. Ibid.

6. Nicholas Varchaver, "What Is Ed Breen Thinking?" *Fortune*, March 20, 2006, *153*(5), 134–139.

7. Ibid.

8. Ibid.

9. Brian Hindo, "Solving Tyco's Identity Crisis," *Business Week*, February 18, 2008, no. 4071, pp. 62–63.

10. Ibid.

11. Ibid.

12. Jennifer Reingold, "Target's Inner Circle," *Fortune*, March 31, 2008, *157*(6), 74–82.

13. Ibid.

14. Ibid., p. 75.

15. Ibid., p. 76.

16. Reingold, "Target's Inner Circle."

17. Ibid.

18. Ibid.

## Chapter 9

1. Christian Caryl, "Why Apple Isn't Japanese," *Newsweek International*, December 10, 2007, *150*(24), 32–34.

2. Ibid.

3. Mark Harper, "Europe Hangs Up on Japanese i-Mode," *Fortune International*, September 6, 2004, *150*(4), 21–22.

4. Michiyo Nakamoto, "NTT DoCoMo Fall Reflects Saturation," *Financial Times*, May 11, 2005, p. 28.

5. Caryl, "Why Apple Isn't Japanese," p. 32.

6. Caryl, "Why Apple Isn't Japanese."

7. Ibid., p. 33.

8. Ibid.

9. Stanley Reed, "The Stealth Oil Giant," *Business Week*, January 14, 2008, no. 4066, p. 40.

10. Reed, "The Stealth Oil Giant," pp. 38–44.

11. Ibid.

12. Ibid.

13. Ibid.

14. Ibid.

15. Ibid.

16. Ibid., p. 40.

17. Reed, "The Stealth Oil Giant."

18. Ibid.

19. Ibid.

**Chapter 10**

1. Adrian Slywotzky, *Value Migration* (Boston: Harvard Business School Press, 1995).

2. Ibid.

3. Ibid.

4. Ibid.

5. Ibid.

6. Ibid.

7. Bruce Nussbaum, "The Power of Design," *Business Week*, May 17, 2004, no. 3883, pp. 86–93.

8. Ibid.

9. Ibid.

10. Ibid.

11. Ibid.

12. Ibid., p. 86.

13. Nussbaum, "The Power of Design."

14. Claire Cain Miller and Parmy Olson, "Tesco's Landing," *Forbes,* June 4, 2007, *179*(12), 116–117.

15. Ibid.

16. Ibid.

17. Ibid., p. 116.

18. Miller and Olson, "Tesco's Landing."

19. Ibid.

20. Ibid.

21. Ibid.

22. Ibid.

23. "How Whirlpool Defines Innovation," *Business Week Online,* March 6, 2006.

24. Ibid.

25. Ibid.

26. Ibid.

27. Ibid.

28. Ibid.

29. Ibid.

30. Ibid.

31. Susan Kitchens, "Farmed-Out Pharma," *Forbes Global,* February 11, 2008, *4*(3), 35–36.

32. Ibid.

33. "Dow and Kuwait Petro: Profit-Margin Play," *Business Week Online,* December 14, 2007.

34. Ibid.

35. Jeffrey Ball and Chip Cummins, "Dow's Plan for Growth Threatened by Scuttled Kuwait Deal," *Wall Street Journal,* December 29, 2008, p. A7.

36. Ibid.

37. Ibid.

38. Michael Freedman, "Good Call," *Forbes*, November 29, 2004, *174*(4), 130.

39. Ibid.

40. Ibid.

41. Ibid.

42. "Sony Ericsson's CEO Talks Strategy," *Business Week Online*, February 12, 2008.

43. Molly Neal, "Ericsson Should Exit the Sony Venture," *Wall Street Journal*, March 20, 2009, p. B3.

44. Ibid.

45. Ibid.

46. Ibid.

47. Ibid.

## Chapter 11

1. Jay Greene, "Microsoft Will Cut Xbox Prices in the U.S.," *Business Week Online*, September 4, 2008.

2. Steve Hamm, "Big Blue Goes for the Big Win," *Business Week*, March 10, 2008, no. 4074, pp. 63–64.

3. Ibid.

4. Ibid.

5. Ibid.

6. Ibid., p. 63.

7. Hamm, "Big Blue."

8. John Simons, "From Scandal to Stardom," *Fortune*, February 18, 2008, *157*(3), 94.

9. Simons, "From Scandal to Stardom," pp. 93–94.

10. Clay Chandler, "Canon's Big Gun," *Fortune*, February 6, 2006, *153*(2), 92–96.

11. Ibid., p. 94.

12. Ibid.

13. Ibid., p. 95.

14. Ian Rowley, Hiroko Tashiro, and Louise Lee, "Can Canon Keep Printing Money?" *Business Week*, September 5, 2005, no. 3949, pp. 48–51.

15. Chandler, "Canon's Big Gun."

16. Ibid.

17. Rowley, Tashiro, and Lee, "Can Canon Keep Printing Money?"

18. Chandler, "Canon's Big Gun."

19. Rowley, Tashiro, and Lee, "Can Canon Keep Printing Money?"

20. Ibid.

21. Ibid.

22. Richard Tomlinson, "Can This Man Focus Philips?" *Fortune International* (Asia edition), March 31, 2003, *147*(6), 44–50.

23. Ibid., p. 44.

24. Ibid., p. 48.

25. Ibid., p. 47.

26. Tomlinson, "Can This Man Focus Philips?"

27. Ibid.

28. Ibid.

29. Ibid.

30. Nelson D. Schwartz, "Lighting Up Philips," *Fortune International* (Europe edition), January 22, 2007, *155*(1), 43–48.

31. Ibid.

32. Ibid., p. 44.

33. Schwartz, "Lighting Up Philips."

34. Tomlinson, "Can This Man Focus Philips?" p. 44.

35. Schwartz, "Lighting Up Philips."

36. Ibid.

# ACKNOWLEDGMENTS

First, I thank Professors Phil Anderson, Hellmut Schutte, Narayan Pant, and Anil Gaba, and Dean Frank Brown of INSEAD. This group was responsible for inviting me to serve as an executive-in-residence at the Asian campus (in Singapore) of that prestigious global graduate business school from January 2006 until January 2009. It was during my time at INSEAD that the thinking behind this book came together.

I also thank Professors Subramanian Rangan and Henri-Claude de Bettignies of INSEAD for inviting me to teach in INSEAD's very successful AVIRA executive leadership course, where I developed many of the examples and distilled the core principles that are discussed in this book.

Next, I thank Wes Neff, who is the president of the Leigh Bureau, a global speakers' bureau. I've worked with Wes since 2002. He helped me launch my first book, *The Fiefdom Syndrome: The Turf Battles That Undermine Careers and Companies—and How to Overcome Them.* Wes was also instrumental in arranging the relationship with McGraw-Hill that resulted in my second book, *Seduced by Success: How the Best Companies Survive the 9 Traps of Winning.* My recent speaking engagements through the Leigh Bureau enabled a lot of the thinking in this book to gel.

Further, I thank Lynn Chu and Glen Hartley of Writers Representatives, LLC, who worked out the contract with John Wiley & Sons for publication of this book. Midge Decter, my fellow board member at the Heritage Foundation, also deserves a thank you for initially putting me in contact with Writers Representatives.

A huge thanks goes to Karen Murphy, Teresa Hennessy, and Mary Garrett of Jossey-Bass/John Wiley & Sons. All three patiently worked with me in editing this book. Karen, as senior editor on the project, was the overall coordinator of all aspects of the book's publication.

Most important, I acknowledge the work of Kim McGee, my administrative assistant here at the Herbold Group, LLC. Kim does it all. This book simply would not have been pulled together on schedule without her constant assistance. She is greatly appreciated.

# ABOUT THE AUTHOR

R obert J. (Bob) Herbold is the managing director of the Herbold Group, LLC, a consulting business focused on profitability, strategic, and operational issues. Herbold also serves on the board of directors of Agilent Technologies and of Neptune Orient Shipping Lines.

Herbold joined Microsoft in 1994 as executive vice president and chief operating officer, retiring in 2001. During his tenure in that position, he was responsible for finance, corporate marketing, market research, manufacturing and distribution, information systems, human resources, and public relations. During his seven years as COO, Microsoft experienced a fourfold increase in revenue and a sevenfold increase in profits. From 2001 to 2003, Herbold worked half-time for Microsoft as executive vice president assisting in government, industry, and customer issues.

Prior to joining Microsoft, Herbold spent twenty-six years at the Procter & Gamble Company. In his last five years with P&G, he served as senior vice president of advertising and information services. In that role, he was responsible for the company's worldwide marketing and brand management operations as well as all marketing-related services, such as media and retail promotion programs. He was also responsible for the worldwide information technology and market research organizations.

Herbold's experiences at Microsoft and Procter & Gamble were the basis of his article in the January 2002 issue of the *Harvard Business Review* titled "Inside Microsoft: Balancing Discipline and Creativity," which focused on how companies can improve their profitability and agility. In 2004, he wrote *The Fiefdom Syndrome: The Turf Battles That Undermine Careers and Companies—and How to Overcome Them* (Random House). His second book, *Seduced by Success: How the Best Companies Survive the 9 Traps of Winning*, was published by McGraw-Hill in 2007.

Herbold has a bachelor of science degree in mathematics from the University of Cincinnati and both a master's degree in mathematics and a doctorate in computer science from Case Western Reserve University. Herbold is a member of the board of trustees of the Heritage Foundation and the Hutchinson Cancer Research Center, and is an adjunct professor in the business school at Nanyang Technological University in Singapore. He is also the president of the Herbold Foundation, which is primarily focused on providing college scholarships to science and engineering students.

# INDEX